T0319470

Lectures on Behavioral Macroeconomics

Lectures on Behavioral Macroeconomics

Paul De Grauwe

Princeton University Press

Princeton and Oxford

Published by Princeton University Press,
41 William Street, Princeton, New Jersey 08540

In the United Kingdom: Princeton University Press,
6 Oxford Street, Woodstock, Oxfordshire OX20 1TW

pup.princeton.edu

Library of Congress Cataloging-in-Publication Data

Grauwe, Paul de.
Lectures on behavioral macroeconomics / Paul De Grauwe.
p. cm.
Includes index.
ISBN 978-0-691-14739-0 (cloth) 1. Macroeconomics. I. Title.
HB172.5.G719 2012
339.01'9–dc23   2012005226

British Library Cataloging in Publication Data is available

Cover illustration: Geometric Cube Background.
© Transfuchsian. Courtesy of Shutterstock.
Jacket design: Kerry Rubenstein

This book has been composed in Times and typeset by T&T Productions Ltd, London

Contents

Preface

Until the eruption of the financial crisis in 2007 it looked as if macroeconomics had achieved the pinnacle of scientific success. The industrial world experienced a time of great macroeconomic stability with low and stable inflation, high and sustained economic growth, and low volatility of many economic and financial variables. Economists were debating the causes of this "Great Moderation" and there was a general consensus that at least part of it was due to the new scientific insights provided by modern macroeconomic theory. This theory embodied the rational agent, who continually optimizes his utility using all available information. In this world where individual agents make no systematic mistakes, stability reigns. Sure, there was a recognition that macroeconomic variables could be subjected to large changes, but these changes always found their source outside the world of these rational agents. If left alone the latter, with the help of efficient markets, would produce their wonderful stabilizing work. The macroeconomy was modeled as a world of rationality and supreme understanding that unfortunately was regularly hit by outside disturbances.

It is no exaggeration to state that the financial and economic upheavals following the crash in the U.S. subprime market have undermined this idyllic view of stability created in a world of fully rational and fully informed agents. These upheavals have also strengthened the view of those who have argued that macroeconomics must take into account departures from rationality, in particular, departures from the assumption of rational expectations.

There is a risk, of course, in trying to model departures from rational expectations. The proponents of the paradigm of the fully informed, rational agent have told us that there are millions of different ways one can depart from rationality. There is thus no hope of coming to any meaningful conclusion once we wander into the world of irrationality. This argument has been very powerful. It has been used to discredit any attempt to depart from the paradigm of the rational and fully informed agent. As a result, many academic researchers have been discouraged from departing from the mainstream macroeconomic theory.

The problem with the objection that "everything becomes possible when we move into the territory of irrationality" is that it is based on the view that there is only one possible formulation of what a rational agent is. This is the formulation now found in mainstream macroeconomic models. It is my contention that one can depart from that particular formulation of rationality without having to wander in the dark world of irrationality.

My intention is to show that once we accept the notion that individuals have cognitive limitations, and thus are not capable of understanding the full complexity of the world (as is routinely assumed in the mainstream macroeconomic models), it is possible to develop models based on a different notion of rationality. I also intend to show that this leads to a richer macroeconomic dynamics that comes closer to the observed dynamics of output and inflation than the one produced by the mainstream macroeconomic models.

I will start by presenting the basic behavioral macroeconomic model that embodies the idea that agents experience cognitive limitations. I will use this model to develop a theory of the business cycle, and I will contrast this theory with the one that is obtained from the mainstream rational expectations macroeconomic model. In chapter 2, I present an analysis of how exogenous shocks are transmitted in a behavioral macroeconomic model. This will then lead to an analysis of monetary policies in a behavioral model (chapters 3 and 4). The next two chapters will discuss the extensions to the basic model. One extension is to introduce asset markets in the model (chapter 5); another extension incorporates a richer menu of forecasting rules than the ones used in the basic model (chapter 6). Finally, in chapter 7, I discuss some empirical issues relating to the question of how well the theoretical predictions of the behavioral model perform when confronted with the data.

Clearly, this is not a definitive book. As the reader will find out, in much of the material that will be presented, there are loose ends and unresolved issues. My intention is to explore new ways of thinking about the macroeconomy; ways of thinking that depart from mainstream thinking, which in my opinion has turned out to be unhelpful in understanding why output and inflation fluctuate as they do in the real world.

I developed many of the ideas in this book through debate with colleagues during seminars and at other occasions. Without implicating them I would like to thank Yunus Aksoy, Tony Atkinson, William Branch, Carl Chiarella, Domenico delli Gatti, Stephan Fahr, Daniel Gros, Richard Harrison, Timo Henckel, Cars Hommes, Romain Houssa, Gerhard Illing, Mordecai Kurz, Pablo Rovira Kaltwasser, Christian Keuschnigg, Alan Kirman, Giovanni Lombardo, Lars Ljungqvist, Patrick Minford, John Muellbauer, Ilbas Pelin, Bruce Preston, Frank Smets, Robert Solow, Leopold von Thadden, David Vines, Mike Wickens, Tony Yates and three anonymous referees.

Lectures on Behavioral Macroeconomics

1

A Behavioral Macroeconomic Model

1.1 Introduction

Capitalism is characterized by booms and busts, by periods of strong growth in output followed by periods of declines in economic growth. Every macroeconomic theory should attempt at explaining these endemic business cycle movements.

Before developing the behavioral model it is useful to present some stylized facts about the cyclical movements of output. In figure 1.1 I show the strong cyclical movements of the output gap in the United States since 1960. These cyclical movements imply that there is strong autocorrelation in the output gap numbers, i.e., the output gap in period t is strongly correlated with the output gap in period $t - 1$. The intuition is that if there are cyclical movements we will observe clustering of good and bad times. A positive (negative) output gap is likely to be followed by a positive (negative) output gap in the next period. This is what we find for the U.S. output gap over the period 1960–2009: the autocorrelation coefficient is 0.94. Similar autocorrelation coefficients are found in other countries.

A second stylized fact about the movements in the output gap is that these are not normally distributed. The evidence for the U.S. is shown in figure 1.2. We find, first, that there is excess kurtosis (kurtosis = 3.62), which means that there is too much concentration of observations around the mean to be consistent with a normal distribution. Second, we find that there are fat tails, i.e., there are more large movements in the output gap than is compatible with the normal distribution. This implies that the business cycle movements are characterized by periods of tranquility interrupted by large positive and negative movements in output, in other words, booms and busts. This also means that if we were basing our forecasts on the normal distribution we would underestimate the probability that in any one period a large increase or decrease in the output gap can occur. Finally, the Jarque–Bera test leads to a formal rejection of normality of the movements in the U.S. output gap series.

The same empirical features have been found in other OECD countries (see Fagiolo et al. 2008, 2009). These authors also confirm that output *growth rates* in most OECD countries are nonnormally distributed, with tails that are much fatter than

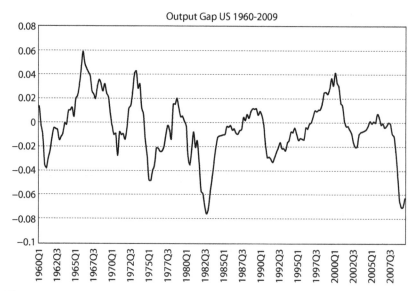

Figure 1.1. *Source:* U.S. Department of Commerce and Congressional Budget Office.

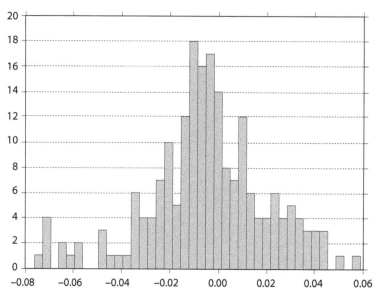

Figure 1.2. Frequency distribution of U.S. output gap (1960–2009): kurtosis, 3.61; Jarque–Bera, 7.17 with p-value = 0.027. *Source:* U.S. Department of Commerce and Congressional Budget Office.

those in a normal distribution. In the empirical chapter 8 additional evidence is provided for other industrialized countries illustrating the same empirical regularities observed for the United States.

One of the purposes of this chapter is to explain this boom and bust characteristic of movements of the business cycle. We will also want to contrast the explanation provided by the behavioral model with the one provided by the mainstream macroeconomic model, which is based on rational expectations.

1.2 The Model

I will use a standard macroeconomic model that in its basic structure is the same as the mainstream new Keynesian model as described in, for example, Galí (2008). In this section I describe this model. In the next I introduce the behavioral assumptions underlying the way agents make forecasts.

The model consists of an aggregate demand equation, an aggregate supply equation, and a Taylor rule.

The aggregate demand equation is specified in the standard way, i.e.,

$$y_t = a_1 \tilde{E}_t y_{t+1} + (1 - a_1) y_{t-1} + a_2(r_t - \tilde{E}_t \pi_{t+1}) + \varepsilon_t, \tag{1.1}$$

where y_t is the output gap in period t, r_t is the nominal interest rate, π_t is the rate of inflation, and ε_t is a white noise disturbance term. $\tilde{E}_t$ is the expectations operator, where the tilde symbol refers to expectations that are not formed rationally. This process will be specified subsequently. I follow the procedure introduced in new Keynesian macroeconomic models of adding a lagged output in the demand equation (see Galí 2008; Woodford 2003). This is usually justified by invoking habit formation. I keep this assumption here as I want to compare the behavioral model with the new Keynesian rational expectations model. However, I will later show that I do not really need this inertia-building device to generate inertia in the endogenous variables.

The aggregate demand equation has a very simple interpretation. Utility-maximizing agents will want to spend more on goods and services today when they expect future income (output gap) to increase and to spend less when the real interest rate increases.

The aggregate supply equation is derived from profit maximization of individual producers (see Galí 2008, chapter 3). In addition, it is assumed that producers cannot adjust their prices instantaneously. Instead, for institutional reasons, they have to wait to adjust their prices. The most popular specification of this price-adjustment mechanism is the Calvo pricing mechanism (Calvo 1983; for a criticism see McCallum 2005). This assumes that in period t a fraction of prices remains unchanged. Under those conditions the aggregate supply equation (which is often referred to as the new Keynesian Philips curve) can be derived as

$$\pi_t = b_1 \tilde{E}_t \pi_{t+1} + (1 - b_1) \pi_{t-1} + b_2 y_t + \eta_t. \tag{1.2}$$

The previous two equations determine the two endogenous variables—inflation and output gap—given the nominal interest rate. The model has to be closed by specifying the way the nominal interest rate is determined. The most popular way to do this has been to invoke the Taylor rule (see Taylor 1993). This rule describes the behavior of the central bank. It is usually written as follows:

$$r_t = c_1(\pi_t - \pi^*) + c_2 y_t + c_3 r_{t-1} + u_t, \tag{1.3}$$

where π^* is the inflation target. Thus the central bank is assumed to raise the interest rate when the observed inflation rate increases relative to the announced inflation target. The intensity with which it does this is measured by the coefficient c_1. Similarly, when the output gap increases the central bank is assumed to raise the interest rate. The intensity with which it does this is measured by c_2. The latter parameter then also tells us something about the ambitions the central bank has to stabilize output. A central bank that does not care about output stabilization sets $c_2 = 0$. We say that this central bank applies strict inflation targeting. Finally, note that, as is commonly done, the central bank is assumed to smooth the interest rate. This smoothing behavior is represented by the lagged interest rate in equation (1.3).

The parameter c_1 is important. It has been shown (see Woodford 2003, chapter 4; Galí 2008) that it must exceed 1 for the model to be stable. This is also sometimes called the "Taylor principle."

Ideally, the Taylor rule should be formulated using a forward-looking inflation variable, i.e., central banks set the interest rate on the basis of their *forecasts* about the rate of inflation. This is not done here in order to maintain simplicity in the model (again see Woodford 2003, p. 257).[1]

It should also be mentioned that another approach to describing the monetary policy of the central bank is to start from a minimization of the loss function and to derive the optimal response of the central bank from this minimization process (see Woodford 2003). This has not been attempted here.

We have added error terms in each of the three equations. These error terms describe the nature of the different shocks that can hit the economy. There are demand shocks, ε_t, supply shocks, η_t, and interest rate shocks, υ_t. We will generally assume that these shocks are normally distributed with mean zero and a constant standard deviation. Agents with rational expectations are assumed to know the distribution of these shocks. It will turn out that this is quite a crucial assumption.

The model consisting of equations (1.1)–(1.3) can be solved under rational expectations. This will be done in Section 1.9. I will call this new Keynesian model with rational expectations the "mainstream model" to contrast it with our behavioral model. I will also occasionally refer to the DSGE model, i.e., the dynamic stochastic general equilibrium model, which has the same features, i.e., new Keynesian wage and price rigidities coupled to rational expectations. In the following sections

---

[1] As is shown in Woodford (2003), forward-looking Taylor rules may not lead to a determinate solution even if the Taylor principle is satisfied.

I specify the assumptions that underlie the forecasting of output and inflation in the behavioral model.

1.3 Introducing Heuristics in Forecasting Output

In the world of rational expectations that forms the basis of the mainstream model, agents are assumed to understand the complexities of the world. In contrast, we take the view that agents have cognitive limitations. They only understand tiny little bits of the world. In such a world agents are likely to use simple rules, heuristics, to forecast the future (see, for example, Damasio 2003; Kahneman 2002; Camerer et al. 2005). In this chapter, a simple heuristic will be assumed. In a later chapter (chapter 5) other rules are introduced. This will be done to study how more complexity in the heuristics affects the results.

Agents who use simple rules of behavior are no fools. They use simple rules only because the real world is too complex to understand, but they are willing to learn from their mistakes, i.e., they regularly subject the rules they use to some criterion of success. There are essentially two ways this can be done. The first one is called statistical learning. It has been pioneered by Sargent (1993) and Evans and Honkapohja (2001). It consists in assuming that agents learn like econometricians do. They estimate a regression equation explaining the variable to be forecasted by a number of exogenous variables. This equation is then used to make forecasts. When new data become available the equation is re-estimated. Thus each time new information becomes available the forecasting rule is updated. The statistical learning literature leads to important new insights (see, for example, Bullard and Mitra 2002; Gaspar et al. 2006; Orphanides and Williams 2004; Milani 2007a; Branch and Evans 2011). However, this approach loads individual agents with a lot of cognitive skills that they may or may not have.[2] I will instead use another learning strategy that can be called "trial-and-error" learning. It is also often labeled "adaptive learning." I will use both labels as synonyms.

Adaptive learning is a procedure whereby agents use simple forecasting rules and then subject these rules to a "fitness" test, i.e., agents endogenously select the forecasting rules that have delivered the highest performance (fitness) in the past. Thus, an agent will start using one particular rule. She will regularly evaluate this rule against the alternative rules. If the former rule performs well, she keeps it. If not, she switches to another rule. In this sense the rule can be called a trial-and-error rule.

This trial-and-error selection mechanism acts as a disciplining device on the kind of rules that are acceptable. Not every rule is acceptable. It has to perform well. What that means will be made clear later. It is important to have such a

---

[2] See the book of Gigerenzer and Todd (1999), which argues that individual agents experience great difficulties in using statistical learning techniques. It has a fascinating analysis on the use of simple heuristics as compared with statistical (regression) learning.

disciplining device, otherwise everything becomes possible. The need to discipline the forecasting rule was also one of the basic justifications underlying rational expectations. By imposing the condition that forecasts must be consistent with the underlying model, the model builder severely limits the rules that agents can use to make forecasts. The adaptive selection mechanism used here plays a similar disciplining role.

There is another important implication of using trial-and-error rules that contrasts a great deal with the rational expectations forecasting rule. Rational expectations implies that agents understand the complex structure of the underlying model. Since there is only one underlying model (there is only one "Truth"), agents understand the same "Truth." They all make exactly the same forecast. This allows builders of rational expectations models to focus on just one "representative agent." In the adaptive learning mechanism that will be used here, this will not be possible because agents can use different forecasting rules. Thus there will be heterogeneity among agents. This is an important feature of the model because, as will be seen, this heterogeneity creates interactions between agents. These interactions ensure that agents influence each other, leading to a dynamics that is absent from rational expectations models.

Agents are assumed to use simple rules (heuristics) to forecast the future output and inflation. The way I proceed is as follows. I assume two types of forecasting rules. A first rule can be called a "fundamentalist" one. Agents estimate the steady-state value of the output gap (which is normalized at 0) and use this to forecast the future output gap. (In a later extension in chapter 7, it will be assumed that agents do not know the steady-state output gap with certainty and only have biased estimates of it.) A second forecasting rule is an "extrapolative" one. This is a rule that does not presuppose that agents know the steady-state output gap. They are agnostic about it. Instead, they extrapolate the previous observed output gap into the future.

The two rules are specified as follows.

(i) The fundamentalist rule is defined by

$$\tilde{E}_t^f y_{t+1} = 0. \tag{1.4}$$

(ii) The extrapolative rule is defined by

$$\tilde{E}_t^e y_{t+1} = y_{t-1}. \tag{1.5}$$

This kind of simple heuristic has often been used in the behavioral finance literature, where agents are assumed to use fundamentalist and chartist rules (see Brock and Hommes 1997; Branch and Evans 2006; De Grauwe and Grimaldi 2006). The rules are simple in the sense that they only require agents to use information they understand, and do not require them to understand the whole picture. Some experimental evidence in support of the two rules (1.4) and (1.5) for inflation forecasts in a new Keynesian model can be found in a paper by Pfajfar and Zakelj (2009).

Thus the specification of the heuristics in (1.4) and (1.5) should not be interpreted as a realistic representation of how agents forecast. Rather is it a parsimonious representation of a world where agents do not know the "Truth" (i.e., the underlying model). The use of simple rules does not mean that the agents are dumb and that they do not want to learn from their errors. I will specify a learning mechanism later in this section in which these agents continually try to correct for their errors by switching from one rule to the other.

The market forecast is obtained as a weighted average of these two forecasts, i.e.,

$$\tilde{E}_t y_{t+1} = \alpha_{f,t} \tilde{E}_t^f y_{t+1} + \alpha_{e,t} \tilde{E}_t^f, \tag{1.6}$$

$$\tilde{E}_t y_{t+1} = \alpha_{f,t} 0 + \alpha_{e,t} y_{t-1}, \tag{1.7}$$

and

$$\alpha_{f,t} + \alpha_{e,t} = 1, \tag{1.8}$$

where $\alpha_{f,t}$ and $\alpha_{e,t}$ are the probabilities that agents use a fundamentalist and an extrapolative rule, respectively.

A methodological issue arises here. The forecasting rules (heuristics) introduced here are not derived at the micro-level and then aggregated. Instead, they are imposed *ex post* on the demand and supply equations. This has also been the approach in the learning literature pioneered by Evans and Honkapohja (2001). Ideally, one would like to derive the heuristics from the micro-level in an environment in which agents experience cognitive problems. Our knowledge about how to model this behavior at the micro-level and how to aggregate it is too sketchy, however. Psychologists and neuroscientists struggle to understand how our brains process information. There is as yet no generally accepted model we could use to model the micro-foundations of information processing in a world in which agents experience cognitive limitations. I have not tried to do so.[3] In the appendix I return to some of the issues related to micro-founding of macroeconomic models.

Selecting the Forecasting Rules

As indicated earlier, agents in our model are not fools. They are willing to learn, i.e., they continually evaluate their forecast performance. This willingness to learn and to change one's behavior is the most fundamental definition of rational behavior. Thus our agents in the model *are* rational, just not in the sense of having rational

---

[3] There are some attempts to provide micro-foundations of models with agents experiencing cognitive limitations, though (see, for example, Kirman 1992; Delli Gatti et al. 2005; Branch and Evans 2011; Branch and McGough 2008).

expectations. We do not use this assumption here because it is an implausible assumption to make about the capacity of individuals to understand the world. Instead our agents are rational in the sense that they learn from their mistakes. The concept of "bounded rationality" is often used to characterize this behavior.

The first step in the analysis then consists in defining a criterion of success. This will be the forecast performance of a particular rule. Thus in this first step, agents compute the forecast performance of the two different forecasting rules as follows:

$$U_{f,t} = -\sum_{k=0}^{\infty} \omega_k [y_{t-k-1} - \tilde{E}_{f,t-k-2} y_{t-k-1}]^2, \qquad (1.9)$$

$$U_{e,t} = -\sum_{k=0}^{\infty} \omega_k [y_{t-k-1} - \tilde{E}_{e,t-k-2} y_{t-k-1}]^2, \qquad (1.10)$$

where $U_{f,t}$ and $U_{e,t}$ are the forecast performances (utilities) of the fundamentalist and extrapolating rules, respectively. These are defined as the mean squared forecasting errors (MSFEs) of the forecasting rules; ω_k are geometrically declining weights. We make these weights declining because we assume that agents tend to forget. Put differently, they give a lower weight to errors made far in the past as compared with errors made recently. The degree of forgetting will turn out to play a major role in our model.

The next step consists in evaluating these forecast performances (utilities). I apply discrete choice theory (see Anderson et al. (1992) for a thorough analysis of discrete choice theory and Brock and Hommes (1997) for the first application in finance) in specifying the procedure agents follow in this evaluation process. If agents were purely rational they would just compare $U_{f,t}$ and $U_{e,t}$ in (1.9) and (1.10) and choose the rule that produces the highest value. Thus under pure rationality, agents would choose the fundamentalist rule if $U_{f,t} > U_{e,t}$, and vice versa. However, things are not so simple. Psychologists have found out that when we have to choose among alternatives we are also influenced by our state of mind. The latter is to a large extent unpredictable. It can be influenced by many things, the weather, recent emotional experiences, etc. One way to formalize this is that the utilities of the two alternatives have a deterministic component (these are $U_{f,t}$ and $U_{e,t}$ in (1.9) and (1.10)) and a random component $\varepsilon_{f,t}$ and $\varepsilon_{e,t}$. The probability of choosing the fundamentalist rule is then given by

$$\alpha_{f,t} = P[U_{f,t} + \varepsilon_{f,t} > (U_{e,t} + \varepsilon_{e,t})]. \qquad (1.11)$$

In words, this means that the probability of selecting the fundamentalist rule is equal to the probability that the stochastic utility associated with using the fundamentalist rule exceeds the stochastic utility of using an extrapolative rule. In order to derive a more precise expression one has to specify the distribution of the random variables $\varepsilon_{f,t}$ and $\varepsilon_{e,t}$. It is customary in the discrete choice literature to assume that these random variables are logistically distributed (see Anderson et al. 1992, p. 35). One then obtains the following expressions for the probability of choosing the fundamentalist rule:

$$\alpha_{f,t} = \frac{\exp(\gamma U_{f,t})}{\exp(\gamma U_{f,t}) + \exp(\gamma U_{e,t})}. \tag{1.12}$$

Similarly the probability that an agent will use the extrapolative forecasting rule is given by

$$\alpha_{e,t} = \frac{\exp(\gamma U_{e,t})}{\exp(\gamma U_{f,t}) + \exp(\gamma U_{e,t})} = 1 - \alpha_{f,t}. \tag{1.13}$$

Equation (1.12) says that as the past forecast performance of the fundamentalist rule improves relative to that of the extrapolative rule, agents are more likely to select the fundamentalist rule for their forecasts of the output gap. Equation (1.13) has a similar interpretation. The parameter γ measures the "intensity of choice." It is related to the variance of the random components $\varepsilon_{f,t}$ and $\varepsilon_{e,t}$. If the variance is very high, γ approaches 0. In that case agents decide to be fundamentalist or extrapolator by tossing a coin and the probability to be fundamentalist (or extrapolator) is exactly 0.5. When $\gamma = \infty$ the variance of the random components is zero (utility is then fully deterministic) and the probability of using a fundamentalist rule is either 1 or 0. The parameter γ can also be interpreted as expressing a willingness to learn from past performance. When $\gamma = 0$ this willingness is zero; it increases with the size of γ.

It should be mentioned here that the probabilities $\alpha_{f,t}$ and $\alpha_{e,t}$ can also be interpreted as the fractions of agents that use a fundamentalist and extrapolative forecasting rule, respectively. This can be seen as follows. Suppose the number of agents is N. Then, if the probability that an agent uses a fundamentalist rule is $\alpha_{f,t}$ on average $\alpha_{f,t} N$ agents will use this rule. Thus the fraction of the total number of agents using this rule is $\alpha_{f,t} N/N = \alpha_{f,t}$. The same holds for $\alpha_{e,t}$. These fractions are determined by the rules (1.12) and (1.13) and are time dependent. This illustrates an important feature of the model, i.e., the heterogeneity of beliefs and their shifting nature over time.

Note also that this selection mechanism is the disciplining device introduced in this model on the kind of rules of behavior that are acceptable. Only those rules that pass the fitness test remain in place. The others are weeded out. In contrast with the disciplining device implicit in rational expectations models, which implies that agents have superior cognitive capacities, we do not have to make such an assumption here.

As argued earlier, the selection mechanism used should be interpreted as a learning mechanism based on "trial and error." When observing that the rule they use performs less well than the alternative rule, agents are willing to switch to the more performing rule. Put differently, agents avoid making systematic mistakes by constantly being willing to learn from past mistakes and to change their behavior. This also ensures that the market forecasts are unbiased.

The mechanism driving the selection of the rules introduces a self-organizing dynamics in the model. It is a dynamics that is beyond the capacity of any one individual in the model to understand. In this sense it is a bottom-up system. It contrasts with the mainstream macroeconomic models in which it is assumed that some or all agents can take a bird's eye view and understand the whole picture. These agents not only understand the whole picture but also use this whole picture to decide about their optimal behavior.

Finally, it is worth mentioning that the selection of the forecasting rules is done according to a standard reinforcement learning model (see, for example, Sutton and Barto 1998). There is a lot of experimental evidence in support of such reinforcement learning models (see, for example, Duffy 2007).

1.4   Heuristics and Selection Mechanism in Forecasting Inflation

Agents also have to forecast inflation. A similar simple heuristics is used as in the case of output gap forecasting, with one rule that could be called a fundamentalist rule and the other an extrapolative rule. (See Brazier et al. (2008) for a similar setup.) We assume an institutional setup in which the central bank announces an explicit inflation target. The fundamentalist rule is then based on this announced inflation target, i.e., agents using this rule have confidence in the credibility of this rule and use it to forecast inflation. Agents who do not trust the announced inflation target use the extrapolative rule, which consists in extrapolating inflation from the past into the future.

The fundamentalist rule will be called an "inflation targeting" rule. It consists in using the central bank's inflation target to forecast future inflation, i.e.,

$$\tilde{E}_t^{\text{tar}} \pi_{t+1} = \pi^*, \tag{1.14}$$

where the inflation target π^* normalized to be equal to 0.

The "extrapolators" are defined by

$$E_t^{\text{ext}} \pi_{t+1} = \pi_{t-1}. \tag{1.15}$$

The market forecast is a weighted average of these two forecasts, i.e.,

$$\tilde{E}_t \pi_{t+1} = \beta_{\text{tar},t} \tilde{E}_t^{\text{tar}} \pi_{t+1} + \beta_{\text{ext},t} \tilde{E}_t^{\text{ext}} \pi_{t+1} \tag{1.16}$$

or

$$\tilde{E}_t \pi_{t+1} = \beta_{\text{tar},t} \pi^* + \beta_{\text{ext},t} \pi_{t-1} \tag{1.17}$$

and

$$\beta_{\text{tar},t} + \beta_{\text{ext},t} = 1. \tag{1.18}$$

The same selection mechanism is used as in the case of output forecasting to determine the probabilities of agents trusting the inflation target and those who do not trust it and revert to extrapolation of past inflation, i.e.,

$$\beta_{\text{tar},t} = \frac{\exp(\gamma U_{\text{tar},t})}{\exp(\gamma U_{\text{tar},t}) + \exp(\gamma U_{\text{ext},t})}, \tag{1.19}$$

$$\beta_{\text{ext},t} = \frac{\exp(\gamma U_{\text{ext},t})}{\exp(\gamma U_{\text{tar},t}) + \exp(\gamma U_{\text{ext},t})}, \tag{1.20}$$

where $U_{\text{tar},t}$ and $U_{\text{ext},t}$ are the forecast performances (utilities) associated with the use of the fundamentalist and extrapolative rules. These are defined in the same way as in (1.9) and (1.10), i.e., they are the negatives of the weighted averages of past squared forecast errors of using fundamentalist (inflation targeting) and extrapolative rules, respectively.

This inflation forecasting heuristics can be interpreted as a procedure of agents to find out how credible the central bank's inflation targeting is. If this is very credible, using the announced inflation target will produce good forecasts and as a result, the probability that agents will rely on the inflation target will be high. If on the other hand the inflation target does not produce good forecasts (compared with a simple extrapolation rule), the probability that agents will use it will be small.

1.5 Solving the Model

The solution of the model is found by first substituting (1.3) into (1.1) and rewriting in matrix notation. This yields

$$\begin{bmatrix} 1 & -b_2 \\ -a_2 c_1 & 1 - a_2 c_2 \end{bmatrix} \begin{bmatrix} \pi_t \\ y_t \end{bmatrix}$$
$$= \begin{bmatrix} 0 & b_1 \\ -a_2 & a_1 \end{bmatrix} \begin{bmatrix} \tilde{E}_t \pi_{t+1} \\ \tilde{E}_t y_{t+1} \end{bmatrix} + \begin{bmatrix} 1-b_1 & 0 \\ 0 & 1-a_1 \end{bmatrix} \begin{bmatrix} \pi_{t-1} \\ y_{t-1} \end{bmatrix}$$
$$+ \begin{bmatrix} 0 \\ a_2 c_3 \end{bmatrix} r_{t-1} + \begin{bmatrix} \eta_t \\ a_2 u_t + \varepsilon_t \end{bmatrix}$$

or

$$A Z_t = B \tilde{E}_t Z_{t+1} + C Z_{t-1} + b r_{t-1} + v_t, \tag{1.21}$$

where bold characters refer to matrices and vectors. The solution for Z_t is given by

$$Z_t = A^{-1}[B \tilde{E}_t Z_{t+1} + C Z_{t-1} + b r_{t-1} + v_t]. \tag{1.22}$$

The solution exists if the matrix A is nonsingular, i.e., if $(1 - a_2 c_2) - a_2 b_2 c_1 \neq 0$. The system (1.22) describes the solution for y_t and π_t given the forecasts of y_t and π_t. The latter have been specified in equations (1.7)–(1.17) and can be substituted into (1.22). Finally, the solution for r_t is found by substituting y_t and π_t obtained from (1.22) into (1.3).

The model has nonlinear features making it difficult to arrive at analytical solutions.[4] That is why we will use numerical methods to analyze its dynamics. In order to do so, we have to calibrate the model, i.e., to select numerical values for the parameters of the model. In Appendix A the parameters used in the calibration exercise are presented. They are based on Galí (2008). The model was calibrated in such a way that the time units can be considered to be months. A sensitivity analysis of the main results to changes in some of the parameters of the model will be presented. The three shocks (demand shocks, supply shocks and interest rate shocks) are independently and identically distributed (i.i.d.) with standard deviations of 0.5%. The Matlab code used for the numerical analysis is also provided in the appendix.

1.6 Animal Spirits, Learning, and Forgetfulness

In this section simulations of the behavioral model in the time domain are presented and interpreted. The upper panel of figure 1.3 shows the time pattern of output produced by the behavioral model given a particular realization of the stochastic i.i.d. shocks. A strong cyclical movement in the output gap can be observed. The autocorrelation coefficient of the output gap is 0.95 (which is very close to 0.94, i.e., the autocorrelation of the output gap that was found in the United States during 1960–2009). The lower panel of figure 1.3 shows a variable called "animal spirits." It represents the evolution of the probabilities that agents extrapolate a positive output gap. As shown earlier, these probabilities can also be interpreted as the fraction of agents using a positive extrapolation rule. Thus, when the probability that agents extrapolate a positive output gap is 1, we will say that the fraction of agents using this rule is 1. When in figure 1.3 the curve reaches 1 all agents are extrapolating a positive output gap; when the curve reaches 0 no agents are extrapolating a positive output gap. In that case they all extrapolate a negative output gap. Thus the curve can also be interpreted as showing the degree of optimism and pessimism of agents who make forecasts of the output gap.

The concept of animal spirits was introduced by Keynes (1936). Keynes defined these as waves of optimism and pessimism of investors that have a self-fulfilling property and that drive the movements of investment and output.[5] As a result of

---

[4] In a way it is paradoxical that it is more difficult to solve the behavioral model than the rational expectations counterpart model. This of course has to do with the fact that the latter is a linear model while the former is nonlinear. This difference in complexity is also related to the fact that the rational expectations model assumes a representative consumer and producer. Solving such a model is then relatively easy because it disregards the complexity that arises from the fact that there is heterogeneity in beliefs.

[5] See Akerlof and Shiller (2009) on the different interpretations of animal spirits. See also Farmer (2006).

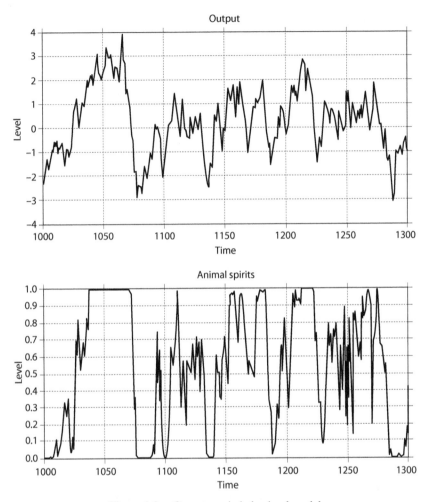

Figure 1.3. Output gap in behavioral model.

the rational expectations revolution, the notion that business cycle movements can be driven by independent waves of optimism and pessimism was discarded from mainstream macroeconomic thinking. Recently, it was given a renewed academic respectability by Akerlof and Shiller (2009).[6] Our model gives a precise definition of these animal spirits. We now show how important these animal spirits are in shaping movements in the business cycle.

---

[6] There is an older literature, which will be discussed in section 1.13, that tried to introduce the notion of animal spirits in macroeconomic models. The idea of animal spirits can also be found in Brock and Hommes (1997).

Combining the information of the two panels in figure 1.3, it can be seen that the model generates endogenous waves of optimism and pessimism (animal spirits). During some periods optimists (i.e., agents who extrapolate positive output gaps) dominate and this translates into above average output growth. These optimistic periods are followed by pessimistic ones when pessimists (i.e., agents who extrapolate negative output gaps) dominate and the growth rate of output is below average. These waves of optimism and pessimism are essentially unpredictable. Other realizations of the shocks (the stochastic terms in equations (1.1)–(1.3)) produce different cycles with the same general characteristics.

These endogenously generated cycles in output are made possible by a self-fulfilling mechanism that can be described as follows. A series of random shocks creates the possibility that one of the two forecasting rules, say, the extrapolating one, has a higher performance (utility), i.e., a lower mean squared forecast error (MSFE). This attracts agents that were using the fundamentalist rule. If the successful extrapolation happens to be a positive extrapolation, more agents will start extrapolating the positive output gap. The "contagion effect" leads to an increasing use of the optimistic extrapolation of the output gap, which in turn stimulates aggregate demand. Optimism is therefore self-fulfilling. A boom is created.

How does a turnaround arise? There are two mechanisms at work. First, there are negative stochastic shocks that may trigger the turnaround. Second, there is the application of the Taylor rule by the central bank. During a boom, the output gap becomes positive and inflation overshoots its target. This leads the central bank to raise the interest rate, thereby setting in motion a reverse movement in output gap and inflation. This dynamics tends to make a dent in the performance of the optimistic extrapolative forecasts. Fundamentalist forecasts may become attractive again, but it is equally possible that pessimistic extrapolation becomes attractive and therefore fashionable again. The economy turns around.

These waves of optimism and pessimism can be understood to be searching (learning) mechanisms of agents who do not fully understand the underlying model but are continually searching for the truth. An essential characteristic of this searching mechanism is that it leads to systematic correlation in beliefs (e.g., optimistic extrapolations or pessimistic extrapolations). This systematic correlation is at the core of the booms and busts created in the model. Note, however, that when computed over a significantly large period of time the average error in the forecasting goes to zero. In this sense, the forecast bias tends to disappear asymptotically.

The results concerning the time path of inflation are shown in figure 1.4. First concentrate on the lower panel of figure 1.4. This shows the fraction of agents using the extrapolator heuristics, i.e., the agents who do not trust the inflation target of the central bank. One can identify two regimes. There is a regime in which the fraction of extrapolators fluctuates around 50%, which also implies that the fraction of forecasters using the inflation target as their guide (the "inflation targeters") is

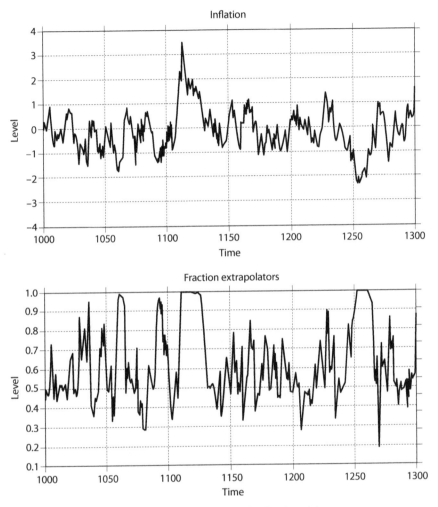

Figure 1.4. Inflation in behavioral model.

around 50%. This is sufficient to maintain the rate of inflation within a narrow band of approximately ±1% around the central bank's inflation target. There is a second regime, however, which occurs when the extrapolators are dominant. During this regime the rate of inflation fluctuates significantly more. Thus the inflation targeting of the central bank is fragile. It can be undermined when forecasters decide that relying on past inflation movements produces better forecast performances than relying on the central bank's inflation target. This can occur quite unpredictably as a result of stochastic shocks in supply and/or demand. We will return to the question of how the central bank can reduce this loss of credibility in chapter 3.

1.7   Conditions for Animal Spirits to Arise

The simulations reported in the previous section assumed a given set of numerical values of the parameters of the model (see the appendix). It was found that for this set of parameter values animal spirits (measured by the movements in the fraction of optimistic extrapolators) emerge and affect the fluctuations of the output gap. The correlation coefficient between the fraction of optimists and the output gap in the simulation reported in figure 1.3 is 0.86. One would like to know how this correlation evolves when one changes the parameter values of the model. I concentrate on two parameter values here, the intensity of choice parameter, γ, and the memory agents have when calculating the performance of their forecasting. This sensitivity analysis will allow us to detect under what conditions animal spirits can arise.

A Willingness to Learn

We first concentrate on the intensity of choice parameter, γ. As will be remembered this is the parameter that determines the intensity with which agents switch from one rule to the other when the performances of these rules change. This parameter is in turn related to the importance of the stochastic component in the utility function of agents. When γ is zero the switching mechanism is purely stochastic. In that case, agents decide about which rule to apply by tossing a coin. They learn nothing from past mistakes. As γ increases they are increasingly sensitive to past performance of the rule they use and are therefore increasingly willing to learn from past errors.

   To check the importance of this parameter γ in creating animal spirits we simulated the model for consecutive values of γ starting from zero. For each value of γ we computed the correlation between the animal spirits and the output gap. We show the results of this exercise in figure 1.5 On the horizontal axis the consecutive values of γ (intensity of choice) are presented. On the vertical axis the correlation coefficient between output gap and animal spirits is shown. We obtain a very interesting result. It can be seen that when γ is zero (i.e., the switching mechanism is purely stochastic), this correlation is zero. The interpretation is that in an environment in which agents decide purely randomly, i.e., they do not react to the performance of their forecasting rule, there are no systematic waves of optimism and pessimism (animal spirits) that can influence the business cycle. When γ increases, the correlation increases sharply. Thus in an environment in which agents learn from their mistakes, animal spirits arise. In other words, one needs a minimum level of rationality (in the sense of a willingness to learn) for animal spirits to emerge and to influence the business cycle. It appears from figure 1.5 that this is achieved with relatively low levels of γ. Thus, surprisingly, animal spirits arise not because agents are irrational. On the contrary, animal spirits can only emerge if agents are sufficiently rational.

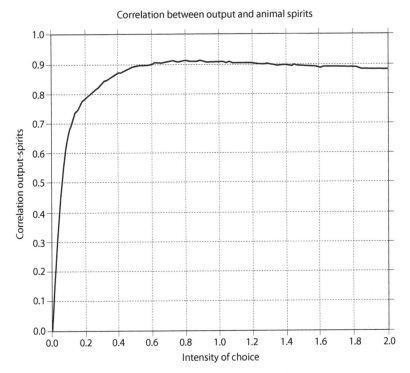

Figure 1.5. Animal spirits and learning.

A Capacity to Forget

When agents test the performance of the forecasting rules they compute past fore-casting errors. In doing so, they apply weights to these past forecast errors. These weights are represented by the parameter ω_k in equations (1.9) and (1.10). We assume that these weights decline as the past recedes. In addition, we assume that these weights decline exponentially. Let us define $\omega_k = (1-\rho)\rho^k$ (and $0 \leqslant \rho \leqslant 1$). We can then rewrite equations (1.9) and (1.10) as follows (if you do not see this, try the reverse, i.e., start from (1.23) and (1.24), do repeated substitutions of $U_{f,t-1}$, $U_{f,t-2}$, etc., and you then find (1.9) and (1.10)):

$$U_{f,t} = \rho U_{f,t-1} - (1-\rho)[y_{t-1} - \tilde{E}_{f,t-2}y_{t-1}]^2, \tag{1.23}$$

$$U_{e,t} = \rho U_{e,t-1} - (1-\rho)[y_{t-1} - \tilde{E}_{e,t-2}y_{t-1}]^2. \tag{1.24}$$

We can now interpret ρ as a measure of the memory of agents. When $\rho = 0$ there is no memory, i.e., only last period's performance matters in evaluating a forecasting rule; when $\rho = 1$ there is infinite memory, i.e., all past errors, however far in the past, obtain the same weight. Since in this case there are infinitely many periods to remember, each period receives the same 0 weight. Values of ρ between 0 and 1 reflect some but imperfect memory. Take as an example $\rho = 0.6$. This number

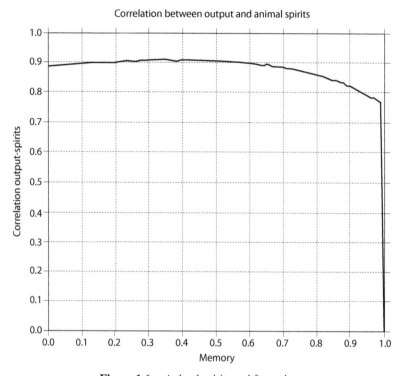

Figure 1.6. Animal spirits and forgetting.

implies that agents give a weight of 0.4 to the last observed error (in period $t - 1$) and a weight of 0.6 to all the errors made in periods beyond the last period.

We performed the same exercise as in the previous section and computed the correlation between animal spirits and the output gap for consecutive values of ρ. The results are shown in figure 1.6. It can be seen that when $\rho = 1$ the correlation is zero. This is the case where agents attach the same weight to all past observations, however far in the past they occur. Put differently, when agents have infinite memory, they forget nothing. Paradoxically, they then also learn nothing from new information. In that case animal spirits do not occur.

Thus one needs some forgetfulness (which is a cognitive limitation) to produce animal spirits. Note that the degree of forgetfulness does not have to be large. For values of ρ below 0.98 the correlations between output and animal spirits are quite high.[7]

This and the previous results lead to an interesting insight. Animal spirits emerge when agents behave rationally (in the sense of a willingness to learn from mistakes)

---

[7] Note that it appears from figure 1.6 that a discontinuity occurs close to $\rho = 1$. This, however, is due to the fact that the figure shows insufficient detail close to $\rho = 1$. The correlation drops to 0 in a continuous manner but this happens at values very close to 1.

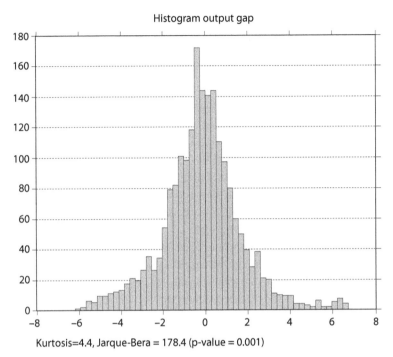

Kurtosis=4.4, Jarque-Bera = 178.4 (p-value = 0.001)

Figure 1.7. Frequency distribution of simulated output gap.

and when they experience cognitive limitations. They do not emerge in a world of either super-rationality or irrationality.

1.8 Two Different Business Cycle Theories: Behavioral Model

How well is our behavioral model capable of mimicking the empirical regularities in the business cycle that we identified in the introduction? This question is answered in this section. In the next section we ask the question of how the mainstream new Keynesian model based on rational expectations (the DSGE model) performs.

Figure 1.3 presented a typical simulation of the output gap obtained in the behavioral model. The autocorrelation coefficient of the output gap obtained in figure 1.3 is 0.95, which is very close to 0.94, i.e., the autocorrelation of the output gap in the United States during 1960–2009 (see the introduction). In addition, our behavioral macroeconomic model produces movements of output that are very different from the normal distribution. We show this by presenting the histogram of the output gaps obtained from figure 1.3. The result is presented in figure 1.7. The frequency distribution of the output gap deviates significantly from a normal distribution. There is excess kurtosis (kurtosis = 4.4), i.e., there is too much concentration of observations around the mean for the distribution to be normal. In addition, there are fat tails. This means that there are too many observations that are very small or very large to be compatible with a normal distribution. We also applied a more formal test of normality, the Jarque–Bera test, which rejected normality. Note that the nonnormality of the distribution of the output gap is produced endogenously by the model, as we feed the model with normally distributed shocks.

This result is not without implications. It implies that when we use the assumption of normality in macroeconomic models we underestimate the probability of large changes. In this particular case, assuming normal distributions tends to underestimate the probability that intense recessions or booms occur. The same is true in finance models that assume normality. These models seriously underestimate the probability of extremely large asset price changes. In other words they underestimate the probability of large bubbles and crashes. To use the metaphor introduced by Nassim Taleb, there are many more black swans than theoretical models based on the normality assumption predict.

It is fine to observe this phenomenon. It is even better to have an explanation for it. Our model provides such an explanation. It is based on the particular dynamics of "animal spirits." We illustrate this in figure 1.8. This shows the frequency distribution of the animal spirits index (defined earlier) which is associated with the frequency distribution of the output gap obtained in figure 1.7. From figure 1.8 we observe that there is a concentration of the animal spirits at the extreme values of 0 and 1 and also in the middle of the distribution (but more spread out). This feature provides the key explanation of the nonnormality of the movements of the output gap.

When the animal spirits index clusters in the middle of the distribution we have tranquil periods. There is no particular optimism or pessimism, and agents use a fundamentalist rule to forecast the output gap. At irregular intervals, however, the economy is gripped by either a wave of optimism or of pessimism. The nature of these waves is that beliefs get correlated. Optimism breeds optimism; pessimism breeds pessimism. This can lead to situations where everybody has become either optimist of pessimist. These periods are characterized by extreme positive of negative movements in the output gap (booms and busts).

From the previous discussion it follows that our behavioral macroeconomic model makes a strong prediction about how the movements of the output gap are distributed. These movements should be nonnormal. This is also what one observes in reality. We come back to the empirical issues in chapter 8.

1.9 Two Different Business Cycle Theories: New Keynesian Model

How well does the new Keynesian rational expectations (DSGE) model perform in mimicking the empirical regularities of the business cycle? In order to answer this question, I used the same model consisting of the aggregate demand equation (1.1), the aggregate supply equation (1.2), and the Taylor rule equation (1.3). The model was solved under rational expectations. This was done as follows.

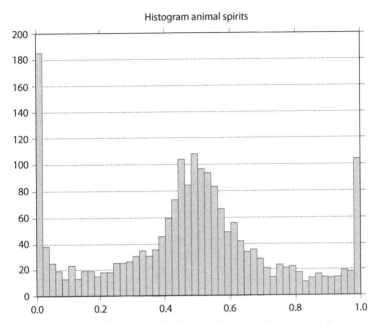

Figure 1.8. Frequency distribution of simulated animal spirits.

The model consisting of equations (1.1)–(1.3) can be written in matrix notation as follows:

$$\begin{bmatrix} 1 & -b_2 & 0 \\ 0 & 1 & -a_2 \\ -c_1 & -c_2 & 1 \end{bmatrix} \begin{bmatrix} \pi_t \\ y_t \\ r_t \end{bmatrix} = \begin{bmatrix} b_1 & 0 & 0 \\ -a_2 & a_1 & 0 \\ 0 & 0 & 0 \end{bmatrix} \begin{bmatrix} E_t\pi_{t+1} \\ E_t y_{t+1} \\ E_t r_{t+1} \end{bmatrix} + \begin{bmatrix} \eta_t \\ \varepsilon_t \\ u_t \end{bmatrix},$$

$$\Omega Z_t = \Phi E_t Z_{t+1} + v_t, \tag{1.25}$$

$$Z_t = \Omega^{-1}[\Phi E_t Z_{t+1} + v_t]. \tag{1.26}$$

There are several ways one can solve for rational expectations (see Minford and Peel 1983; Walsh 2003). Here I will use numerical methods to solve the system mainly because the behavioral model that was used earlier is highly nonlinear (in contrast with the rational expectations version of the model, which is linear) necessitating the use of numerical solution techniques. I use the Binder–Pesaran procedure (Binder and Pesaran 1996). The Matlab code is provided in appendix. The numerical values of the parameters are the same as those used for the behavioral model (see appendix). They are based on values commonly used in these models (see Galí 2008, p. 52).

I show the movements of the simulated output gap in figure 1.9. The upper panel shows the output gap in the time domain and the lower panel in the frequency domain. The autocorrelation in the output gap is 0.77, which is significantly lower than in the observed data (for the United States we found 0.94). In addition, these

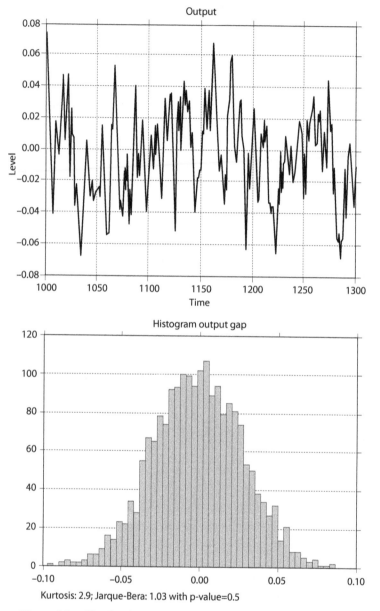

Figure 1.9. Simulated output gap in extended new Keynesian model.

output gap movements are normally distributed (see lower panel). We could not reject that the distribution is normal. Thus, it appears that the simple new Keynesian rational expectations model which is fed with random disturbances is not capable of representing two important empirical features. These are the cyclical nature of output gap movements and nonnormality of its distribution.

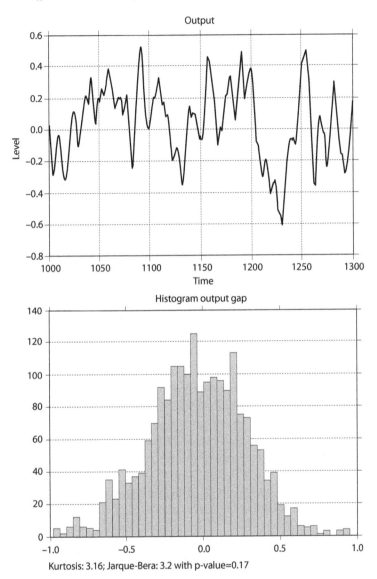

Figure 1.10. Simulated output gap in extended
new Keynesian model and autocorrelated errors.

The next step in making this model more empirically relevant has consisted in adding autocorrelation in the error terms. This is now the standard procedure in DSGE models (see Smets and Wouters 2003). We do the same with our version of the new Keynesian rational expectations model and assume that the autocorrelation of the error terms in the equations (1.1)–(1.3) is equal to 0.9. The result of this assumption is shown in the simulations of the output gap in figure 1.10. We now obtain movements of the output gap that resemble real-life movements. The autocorrelation of the output gap is now 0.98, which is very close to the observed number of 0.94 in the postwar U.S. output gap. We still cannot reject normality though (see the Jarque–Bera test). This is a problem that DSGE models have not been able to solve.

Thus, in order to mimic business cycle movements, the new Keynesian rational expectations (DSGE) model builders have had recourse to introducing autocorrelation in the error terms (the shocks that hit the economy). This trick has allowed DSGE models to closely fit observed data (see Smets and Wouters 2003). This success has been limited to the first and second moments of the movements of output, but not to the higher moments (kurtosis, fat tails). The latter failure has the implication that in order to explain a large movement in output (e.g., a deep recession or a strong boom) DSGE models have to rely on large unpredictable shocks.

There are two problems with this theory of the business cycle implicit in the DSGE models.

First, business cycles are not the result of an endogenous dynamics. They occur as a result of exogenous shocks and slow transmission of these shocks (because of wage and price rigidities). Put differently, the DSGE models picture a world populated by rational agents who are fully informed. In such a world there would never be business cycles. The latter arise because of exogenous disturbances and of constraints on agents' ability to react instantaneously to these shocks. Thus a given shock will produce ripple effects in the economy, i.e., cyclical movements.

Thus, the DSGE models explain the large booms and busts that are regularly observed in capitalist economies by large outside shocks. The macroeconomy is a peaceful world in which agents continually optimize. However, sometimes this peaceful world is hit by large exogenous disturbances that are then transmitted into the macroeconomy.

This is not a very satisfactory theory of the business cycle.[8] It leads to the question of why the world outside the macroeconomy is characterized by nonnormally distributed shocks, while the macroeconomy itself does not produce such shocks. The macroeconomist in the mainstream world is therefore condemned to ask other scientists why these large shocks occur. He has no theory capable of explaining these.

A second problem is methodological. When the new Keynesian model is tested empirically, the researcher finds that there is a lot of the output dynamics that is not predicted by the model. This unexplained dynamics is then to be found in the error term. So far so good. The next step taken by DSGE modelers is to conclude that these errors (typically autocorrelated) should be considered to be exogenous shocks.

---

[8] There is a long tradition in economics of developing endogenous business cycle theories (e.g., Hicks 1950; Goodwin 1951). This has been completely abandoned in modern macroeconomics.

The problem with this approach is that it is scientifically questionable. When the DSGE modeler finds a dynamics not predicted by the model, he decides that the new Keynesian rational expectations model must nevertheless be right (because there can be no doubt that individual agents are rational) and that thus the deviation between the observed dynamics and the one predicted by the model must come from outside the model.

1.10 Uncertainty and Risk

Frank Knight, a famous professor of economics at the University of Chicago before World War II, introduced the distinction between risk and uncertainty in his book *Risk, Uncertainty and Profits*, published in 1921. Risk according to Knight is quantifiable. It has to do with events that have a probability of occurrence that can be represented by a statistical distribution. As a result, we can compute the probability that these events occur with great precision. The reason we can do this is that there is some regularity in the occurrence of these events and lots of data to detect this regularity. In contrast, uncertainty does not allow for such quantification because of a lack of regularity and/or an insufficiency of data to detect these regularities.

The mainstream macroeconomic models based on rational expectations (including the DSGE models) only allow for risk. In these models agents are capable of making probabilistic statements about all future shocks based on quantifiable statistical distributions obtained from the past. Thus in the DSGE models agents know, for example, that in any period there is a probability of, say, 10% that a negative supply shock of −5% will occur. In fact, they can tabulate the probability of all possible supply shocks, and all possible demand shocks. This is certainly an extraordinary assumption.

The frequency distribution of the output gap presented in figure 1.7 suggests that although the distribution is nonnormal, there is enough regularity in the distribution for individual agents to use in order to make probabilistic predictions. This regularity, however, appears only because of a large amount of periods (2000) in the simulation exercise. Assuming that one period corresponds to one month, we can see that the frequency distribution is obtained using 170 years of observations. In most developed countries today the maximum number of years for which we have output gap data is about 40–50, a quarter of the number of observations used to construct the frequency distribution in figure 1.7.

The question that then arises is, how reliable are frequency distributions of the output gap obtained from much shorter periods? In order to answer this question we ran simulations of the behavioral model over short periods (400, corresponding to approximately 40 years). For each 400-period simulation we computed the frequency distribution of the output gap. The result is presented in figure 1.11. We observe that the frequency distributions of the output gap obtained in different 400-period simulations look very different. All exhibit excess kurtosis but the degree of

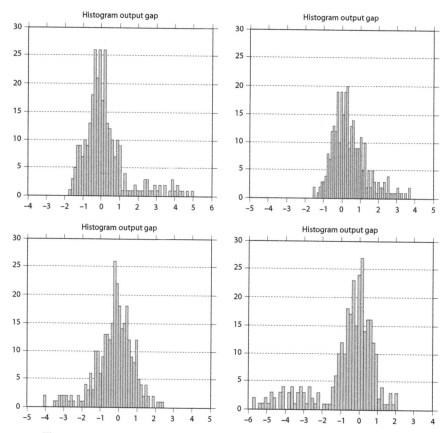

Figure 1.11. Frequency distribution of output gap in 400-period simulations.

excess kurtosis varies a great deal. In all cases there is evidence of fat tails, but the exact shape varies a lot. In some 400-period simulations there are only positive fat tails, in others only negative fat tails. In still other simulations fat tails appear on both sides of the distributions.

This suggests that if our model of animal spirits is the right representation of the real world, observations over periods of approximately 40 years are by far insufficient to detect regularities in the statistical distributions of important variables as the output gap that can be used to make probabilistic statements about this variable. Thus, our behavioral model comes close to representing a world in which uncertainty rather than risk prevails at the macroeconomic level. This contrasts with the standard rational expectations macroeconomic models in which there is only risk and no uncertainty.

Our simulations using the behavioral model suggest that over 40-year periods we should see different frequency distributions for the output gap. But given our limited historical sample (just one historical frequency distribution), it is difficult to test for this result. Put differently, how do we know that uncertainty is more relevant than risk in macroeconomic modeling? We will come back to this question in the empirical chapter. There it will be shown that using evidence of more than one country, the empirically observed frequency distributions obtained for relatively short periods have very different shapes and forms, making it difficult to draw statistical inferences. Thus, as will be shown, the empirical evidence suggests that it is uncertainty rather than risk that prevails in macroeconomic reality. That is also what our behavioral model tells us.

One could also argue that the difference we have detected here between uncertainty and risk is a matter of degree rather than of essence. In our model uncertainty is transformed into measurable risk if the number of observations becomes large enough. This criticism is undoubtedly true. In fact there has always been a dual interpretation of the difference between uncertainty and risk. The first one is more narrow and is also found in our model: uncertainty arises because we lack sufficient data to make statistical inferences. The second one considers the difference to be qualitative in nature, i.e., the increase in data points does not improve the capacity for making statistical inferences, because some phenomena do not lend themselves to measurement (at least with our present state of understanding of these phenomena). Our model gives substance to the first interpretation of the difference between uncertainty and risk. It does not do justice to the second interpretation.

1.11 Credibility of Inflation Targeting and Animal Spirits

In the previous sections we identified the conditions in which animal spirits, i.e., self-fulfilling waves of optimism and pessimism, can arise. We argued that when animal spirits prevail, uncertainty in Frank Knight's sense is created. Our implicit assumption was that the inflation target announced by the central bank is not 100% credible. This imperfect credibility leads agents to be skeptical and to continually test the resolve of the central bank. We showed that in such an environment animal spirits can arise.

In this section we ask the following question. Suppose the inflation target can be made 100% credible. What does such a regime imply for the emergence of animal spirits? We ask this question not because we believe that such a perfect credibility can be achieved, but rather to analyze the conditions under which animal spirits can arise.

We analyze this question in the following way. Equations (1.14) and (1.15) define the forecasting rules agents use in an environment of imperfect credibility. In such an environment, agents will occasionally be skeptical about the announced inflation target. In that case they cease to use the inflation target to forecast inflation and revert to an extrapolative rule. In a perfectly credible inflation targeting regime, agents have no reason to be skeptical and will therefore always use the announced target as the basis for their forecast. Thus in a perfectly credible regime, agents only use rule (1.14) and there is no switching. The market forecast of inflation (equation (1.17)) now simplifies to

$$\tilde{E}_t \pi_{t+1} = \pi^*$$

and the switching equations (1.19) and (1.20) disappear. The rest of the model is unchanged.

We simulated this version of the model using the same techniques as in the previous sections. We show some of the results in figure 1.12 and compare them with the results obtained in the regime of imperfect credibility of inflation targeting analyzed in the previous section.

The contrast in the results is quite striking. When inflation targeting is perfectly credible, animal spirits are weak. This can be seen from the fact that the animal spirits index does not show a concentration of observations at the extreme values of 1 (extreme optimism) and 0 (extreme pessimism). This contrasts very much with the imperfect credibility case. This difference in occurrence of animal spirits has the effect of eliminating the fat tails in the frequency distribution of the output gap and of inflation. In fact both distributions are now normal with a kurtosis around 3. The Jarque–Bera test cannot reject the hypothesis that the distributions of output gap and inflation are normal in the perfect credibility case. The contrast with the distributions obtained in the imperfect credibility case is striking: these exhibit fat tails and excess kurtosis.

Thus when inflation targeting is perfectly credible, periods of intense booms and busts produced by the existence of animal spirits do not occur. In addition, Knightian uncertainty is absent. The normal distribution of output gap and inflation allows agents to make reliable probabilistic statements about these variables. Where does this result come from? The answer is that when inflation targeting is perfectly credible, the central bank does not have to care about inflation because inflation remains close to the target most of the time. As a result, the interest rate instrument can be used to stabilize output most of the time. Thus when animal spirits are optimistic and tend to create a boom, the central bank can kill the boom by raising the interest rate. It can do the opposite when animal spirits are pessimistic. Put differently, in the case of perfect credibility the central bank is not put into a position where it has to choose between inflation and output stabilization. Inflation stability is achieved automatically. As a result, it can concentrate its attention on stabilizing output. This then "kills" the animal spirits.

A fully credible inflation-targeting regime produces wonderfully stabilizing results on output and inflation movements. How can a central bank achieve such a regime of full credibility of its announced inflation target? A spontaneous answer is that this could be achieved more easily by a central bank that only focuses on stabilizing the rate of inflation and stops worrying about stabilizing output. Thus by following a strict inflation targeting regime a central bank is, so one may think,

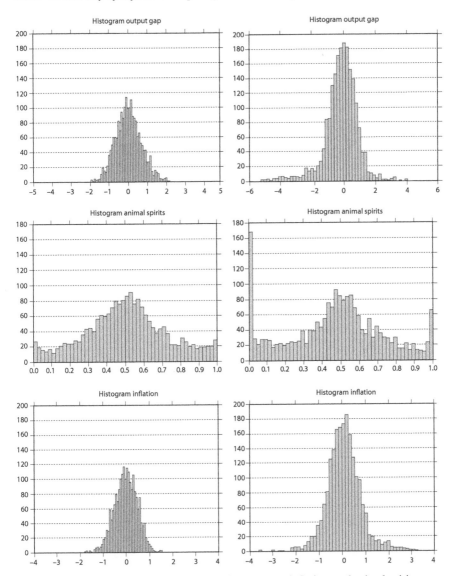

Figure 1.12.   Frequency distribution of output gap, inflation, and animal spirits.

more likely to reach full credibility. We checked whether this conclusion is correct in the following way. We simulated the model assuming that the central bank sets the output coefficient in the Taylor rule equal to zero. Thus this central bank does not care at all about output stabilization and only focuses on the inflation target. Will such a central bank, applying strict inflation targeting, come close to full credibility? We show the result of simulating the model under strict inflation targeting in figure 1.13. The answer is immediately evident. The frequency distribution of

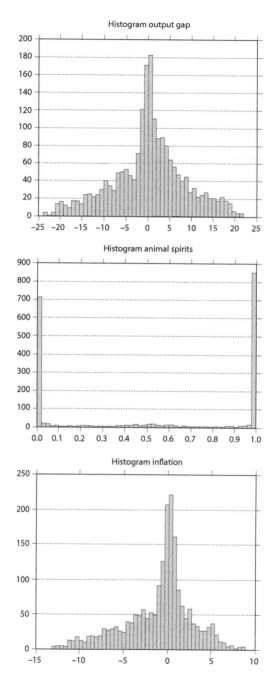

Figure 1.13.   Frequency distribution of output gap, animal spirits,
and inflation with strict inflation targeting.

output gap shows extreme deviations from the normal distribution with very fat tails, suggesting large booms and busts. Even more remarkably, we find the same feature in the frequency distribution of the rate of inflation that now shows large deviations from the target (normalized at 0).

Thus strict inflation targeting dramatically fails to bring us closer to full inflation credibility. The reason why this is so, is that the power of the animal spirits is enhanced. This can be seen by the middle graph in figure 1.13. We now see that most of the time the economy is gripped by either extreme optimism or extreme pessimism. This tends to destabilize not only the output gap but also the rate of inflation. Thus, strict inflation targeting instead of bringing us closer to the nirvana of perfect credibility moves us away from it. We will come back to this issue in chapter 3, where we analyze the trade-offs between inflation and output variability in a behavioral macroeconomic model.

This result stands in stark contrast with the results obtained in the mainstream rational expectations model (Woodford 2003; Galí 2008). In these models strict inflation targeting, while generally not optimal because of the existence of wage and price inertia, has important stabilizing features. As a result, strict inflation targeting pretty much approximates the optimal policy in the standard model (see Galí 2008, p. 11).

1.12 Different Types of Inertia

The behavioral and rational expectations macroeconomic models lead to very different views on the nature of business cycle. Business cycle movements in the rational expectations (DSGE) models arise as a result of exogenous shocks (in productivity, preferences, policy regime) and lags in the transmission of these shocks to output and inflation. Thus inertia in output and inflation are the result of the lagged transmission of exogenous shocks. In addition, as was pointed out in Section 1.9, DSGE modelers have routinely added autoregressive exogenous shocks, thereby importing a dynamics that is not explained by the model. As a result, one could call the business cycles introduced in the DSGE model exogenously created phenomena.

In contrast, the behavioral model presented here is capable of generating inertia, and business cycles, without imposing lags in the transmission process and without the need to impose autocorrelation in the error terms. This could be called endogenous inertia.[9] This is shown by presenting simulations of output and animal spirits in the absence of lags in the transmission process in the demand and the supply equations. This is achieved by setting the parameters of the forward-looking variables $a_1 = 1$ in equation (1.1) and $b_1 = 1$ in equation (1.2). The results are presented in figure 1.14. We observe similar business cycle movements in output

---

[9] A similar informational inertia is found in Ball et al. (2005) and Mankiw and Reis (2002).

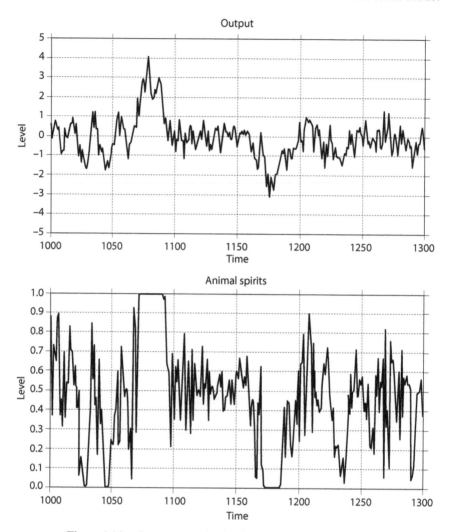

Figure 1.14. Output gap and animal spirits in model without lags.

that are highly correlated to animal spirits as in figure 1.3. The correlation between output and animal spirits now is 0.71, which is somewhat lower than when lags in the transmission process were assumed (figure 1.3). This correlation, however, remains significant and is the main driving force behind the output fluctuations.

The inertia obtained in the behavioral model could also be called informational inertia. In contrast to the rational expectations model, agents in the behavioral model experience an informational problem. They do not fully understand the nature neither of the shock nor of its transmission. They try to understand it by applying a trial-and-error learning rule, but they never succeed in fully understanding the complexity of the world. This cognitive problem then creates the inertia in output and prices. Thus one obtains very different theories of the business cycles in the two models.[10]

1.13 Animal Spirits in the Macroeconomic Literature

The behavioral model presented in this section is not the first one to formalize the idea of animal spirits, i.e., expectations-driven business cycle movements. In fact there is a very large literature that has done so in various ways. In this section we compare our approach with these different strands of the literature.

First, there is an important strand of literature producing models with sunspot equilibria. This literature started with Shell (1977) and Azariadis (1981), and includes Azariadis and Guesnerie (1986). Models with sunspot equilibria are found both in the RBC framework (see Benhabib and Farmer 1994; Farmer and Guo 1994) as in the new Keynesian framework (Clarida et al. 1999). In these models there are multiple RE solutions, which include "self-fulfilling" solutions that depend on extraneous variables ("sunspots"). These models provide for a fully rational way to model animal spirits, implementing the basic insights of Keynes (1936).

A very similar strand of literature is provided by models generating global indeterminacies. Howitt and McAfee (1992), Evans et al. (1998), and Evans and Honkapohja (2001) develop models with externalities that lead to multiple steady states. These papers exhibit equilibria with random switching between high and low activity steady states (or, in the Evans–Honkapohja–Romer paper, between high and low growth rates). The rational expectations solutions in these models depend on an exogenous two-state Markov variable that acts to coordinate expectations and triggers the shifts between high (optimistic) and low (pessimistic) states.[11]

The common characteristics of these multiple equilibria models is an exogenous process that leads to switches between these different equilibria. Thus, when "animal spirits" arise in these models, they are exogenously driven. The model presented in the present chapter differs from these multiple equilibria models in that it does not rely on extraneous "sunspots." The economic fluctuations are driven instead by the intrinsic random (white noise) shocks of the model. These white noise shocks are transformed into "animal spirits" in an endogenous way.

---

[10] Critics of the heuristic model presented here may argue that the comparison between the rational and the behavioral model is unfair for the rational model. Indeed, the heuristic model generates inertia because the evaluation and selection process of the different heuristics is backward looking. This is the reason why the behavioral model does not need lags in the transmission process to generate inertia. However, it can be argued that this evaluation and selection process can only be backward looking, and as a result, the lags that are present in the behavioral model are within the logic of that model. This contrasts with the lags introduced in the rational model: they come from outside the model. See Milani (2007b), who makes a similar point by contrasting rational expectations models with learning models.

[11] It should be noted that in each of these models fluctuations can also arise as the outcome of a boundedly rational learning process. Another attempt to produce endogenous fluctuations is to be found in Kurz (1994) and Kurz and Motolese (2011).

The latter is also the case in Evans and Honkapohja (2001, chapter 14) in which the fluctuations are driven by productivity shocks, with the learning rule leading to occasional shifts between equilibria. However, our model differs from this and the previous models in that it does not have multiple equilibria under rational expectations. Instead, the multiplicity is the result of the restricted list of forecast rules from which the agents can choose.

Our model comes closest to Branch and Evans (2007), who also use a discrete choice framework inside a simple monetary model and who find regime-switching behavior driven by the shocks in the model. The shifts in expectations, as agents occasionally move from pooling on one forecast rule to pooling on the other rule, is a kind of self-fulfilling phenomenon. The similarity with our model is that in the Branch and Evans (2007) model there is a unique equilibrium under rational expectations, but because agents must choose between two misspecified models, there are multiple equilibria (of a type that the authors carefully define). Under real-time updating of the discrete-choice type, this leads to regime-switching behavior over time. However, in Branch and Evans (2007) the switching is between high and low volatility regimes, whereas in our model it is also between high and low activity states, generating business cycle effects that are of first order.

1.14 Conclusion

In mainstream new Keynesian rational expectations models, large disturbances in output and prices only occur if there are large exogenous shocks in demand and supply or in the policy environment. Without these exogenous shocks rational and superbly informed agents peacefully optimize. They may have to wait a little to do this because of wage and price rigidities but in the end they satisfy their desired plans. Only tornado-like external shocks can disturb this peaceful environment.

The model presented in this chapter is very different. It is capable of generating large movements in output (booms and busts) without having to rely on large exogenous shocks. We assumed throughout this chapter that the exogenous disturbances are normally distributed. Yet the behavioral model is capable of generating a statistical distribution of output movements that is not normally distributed and that has fat tails. These are large movements in output that occur with a higher probability than the normal distribution predicts.

The underlying mechanism that produces these movements are the waves of optimism and pessimism ("animal spirits") generated endogenously and that have a self-fulfilling property. We found that periods of tranquility during which the animal spirits remain quiet are followed (unpredictably) by periods when the animal spirits take over, i.e., large movements of optimism or pessimism lead the economy to a period of boom and bust.

Thus our behavioral model produces a theory of the business cycle that is very different from the standard new Keynesian rational expectations (DSGE) model.

In the latter model the booms and busts in output are always the result of large exogenous shocks. In the DSGE world, the financial crisis that started in August 2007 and the intense recession that followed it were produced by a sudden exogenous shock in 2007 that, as a tornado, created havoc in the financial markets and in the macroeconomy. In fact, it is now standard practice for DSGE modelers to simulate the consequences of the financial crisis on the economy by introducing an exogenous increase in risk aversion (and thus the risk premium).[12] In contrast, the behavioral model developed in this chapter is capable of producing endogenous booms and busts. This model leads to the view that the bust of 2007–8 was the result of a boom generated by excessive optimism prior to that date.

Throughout this chapter we assumed small and normally distributed shocks to highlight the potential of the model to generate large and nonnormally distributed movements in output. In the real world, large exogenous shocks do occur. As a result, the movements in output and prices will always be a mix of internally generated dynamics and outside disturbances. In the next chapter we therefore analyze how external shocks are transmitted in the behavioral model.

---

[12] Interestingly, this is also the view of major bankers when they were questioned during hearings in the U.S. Congress in January 2010. These bankers used metaphors such as "a perfect storm" and "a tornado" to describe the causes of the financial crisis.

Appendix 1: Parameter Values of the Calibrated Model

Behavioral Model

pstar=0;	%the central bank's inflation target
a1=0.5;	%coefficient of expected output in output equation
a2=-0.2;	%a is the interest elasticity of output demand
b1=0.5;	%b1 is coefficient of expected inflation in inflation equation
b2=0.05;	%b2 is coefficient of output in inflation equation
c1=1.5;	%c1 is coefficient of inflation in Taylor equation
c2=0.5;	%c2 is coefficient of output in Taylor equation
c3=0.5;	%interest smoothing parameter in Taylor equation
beta=1;	%fixed divergence in beliefs
delta=2;	%variable component in divergence of beliefs
gamma=1;	%intensity of choice parameter
sigma1=0.5;	%standard deviation shocks output
sigma2=0.5;	%standard deviation shocks inflation
sigma3=0.5;	%standard deviation shocks Taylor
rho=0.5;	%rho measures the speed of declining weights in mean squares errors (memory parameter)

Rational Model

pstar=0;	%the central bank's inflation target
a1=0.5;	%coefficient of expected output in output equation
a2=-0.2;	%a is the interest elasticity of output demand
b1=0.5;	%b1 is coefficient of expected inflation in inflation equation
b2=0.05;	%b2 is coefficient of output in inflation equation
c1=1.5;	%c1 is coefficient of inflation in Taylor equation
c2=0.5;	%c2 is coefficient of output in Taylor equation
c3=0.5;	%interest smoothing parameter in Taylor equation
sigma1=0.5;	%standard deviation shocks output
sigma2=0.5;	%standard deviation shocks inflation
sigma3=0.5;	%standard deviation shocks Taylor

Appendix 2: Matlab Code for the Behavioral Model

```
%% Parameters of the model
mm=1;              %switching parameter gamma in Brock Hommes
pstar=0;           %the central bank's inflation target
eprational=0;      %if all agents have rational forecast of inflation this
                     parameter is 1
epextrapol=0;      %if all agents use inflation extrapolation this parameter is 1
a1=0.5;            %coefficient of expected output in output equation
a2=-0.2;           %a is the interest elasticity of output demand
b1=0.5;            %b1 is coefficient of expected inflation in inflation equation
b2=0.05;           %b2 is coefficient of output in inflation equation
c1=1.5;            %c1 is coefficient of inflation in Taylor equation
c2=0.5;            %c2 is coefficient of output in Taylor equation
c3=0.5;            %interest smoothing parameter in Taylor equation
A=[1 -b2;-a2*c1 1-a2*c2];
B=[b1 0;-a2 a1];
C=[1-b1 0;0 1-a1];
T=2000;
TI=250;
K=50;              %length of period to compute divergence
sigma1=0.5;        %standard deviation shocks output
sigma2=0.5;        %standard deviation shocks inflation
sigma3=0.5;        %standard deviation shocks Taylor
rho=0.5;           %rho in mean squares errors
rhoout=0.0;        %rho in shocks output
rhoinf=0.0;        %rho in shocks inflation
rhotayl=0.0;       %rho in shocks Taylor
rhoBH=0.0;
epfs=pstar;        %forecast inflation targeters
p=zeros(T,1);
y=zeros(T,1);
plagt=zeros(T,1);
ylagt=zeros(T,1);
r=zeros(T,1);
epf=zeros(T,1);
epc=zeros(T,1);
ep=zeros(T,1);
ey=zeros(T,1);
CRp=zeros(T,1);
FRp=zeros(T,1);
```

```
alfapt=zeros(T,1);
eyfunt=zeros(T,1);
CRy=zeros(T,1);
FRy=zeros(T,1);
alfayt=zeros(T,1);
anspirits=zeros(T,1);
epsilont=zeros(T,1);
etat=zeros(T,1);
ut=zeros(T,1);
%%%%%%%%%%
% behavioral model %
%%%%%%%%%%
   alfap=0.5;
   alfay=0.5;
   K1=K+1;
for t=2:T
   epsilont(t)=rhoout*epsilont(t-1) + sigma1*randn;
                        %shocks in output equation (demand shock)
   etat(t)= rhoinf*etat(t-1) + sigma2*randn;
                        %shocks in inflation equation (supply shock)
   ut(t)=rhotayl*ut(t-1) + sigma3*randn;
                        %shocks in Taylor rule (interest rate shock)
   epsilon=epsilont(t);
   eta=etat(t);
   u=ut(t);
   shocks=[eta;a2*u+epsilon];
   epcs=p(t-1);
   if eprational=1;
      epcs=pstar;
   end
   eps=alfap*epcs+(1-alfap)*epfs;
   if epextrapol=1;
      eps=p(t-1);
   end
   eychar=y(t-1);
   eyfun=0+randn/2;
   eyfunt(t)=eyfun;
   eys=alfay*eychar+(1-alfay)*eyfun;
   forecast=[eps;eys];
   plag=p(t-1);
   ylag=y(t-1);
```

```
rlag=r(t-1);
lag=[plag;ylag];
smooth=[0;a2*c3];
D=B*forecast + C*lag + smooth*rlag + shocks;
X=A\D;
p(t)= X(1,1);
y(t)= X(2,1);
r(t)= c1*p(t)+c2*y(t)+c3*r(t-1)+u;
if square=1;
   r(t)= c1*(p(t))^2+c2*y(t)+c3*r(t-1)+u;
end
plagt(t)=p(t-1);
ylagt(t)=y(t-1);
CRp(t)=rho*CRp(t-1) - (1-rho)*(epcs-p(t))^2;
FRp(t)=rho*FRp(t-1) - (1-rho)*(epfs-p(t))^2;
CRy(t)=rho*CRy(t-1) - (1-rho)*(eychar-y(t))^2;
FRy(t)=rho*FRy(t-1) - (1-rho)*(eyfun-y(t))^2;
alfap=rhoBH*alfapt(t-1) + (1-rhoBH)
             *exp(mm*CRp(t))/(exp(mm * CRp(t)) + exp(mm * FRp(t)));
alfay=rhoBH*alfayt(t-1) + (1-rhoBH)
             *exp(mm*CRy(t))/(exp(mm * CRy(t)) + exp(mm * FRy(t)));
alfapt(t)=alfap;
alfayt(t)=alfay;
if eychar>0;
   anspirits(t)=alfay;
end
if eychar<0;
     anspirits(t)=1-alfay;
end
end
autocory=corrcoef(y,ylagt);
autocorp=corrcoef(p,plagt);
coroutputanimal=corr(y,anspirits);
%% mean, median, max, min, standard deviation, kurtosis
Kurt=kurtosis(y);
%% Jarque-Bera test
[jb,pvalue,jbstat]=jbtest(y,0.05);
```

Appendix 3: Some Thoughts on Methodology in Mainstream Macroeconomics

One of the surprising developments in macroeconomics is the systematic incorporation of the paradigm of the utility-maximizing forward-looking and fully informed agent into macroeconomic models. This development started with the rational expectations revolution of the 1970s, which taught us that macroeconomic models can be accepted only if agents' expectations are consistent with the underlying structure of the model. The real business cycle (RBC) theory introduced the idea that macroeconomic models should be "micro-founded," i.e., should be based on dynamic utility maximization (Kydland and Prescott 1982). While RBC model had no place for price rigidities and other inertia (which is why it is sometimes called the new classical model), the new Keynesian school systematically introduced rigidities of different kinds into similar micro-founded models. These developments occurred in the ivory towers of academia for several decades until in recent years these models were implemented empirically in such a way that they have now become tools of analysis in the boardrooms of central banks. The most successful implementation of these developments are to be found in the dynamic stochastic general equilibrium models (DSGE models) that are increasingly used in central banks for policy analysis (see Smets and Wouters 2003; Christiano et al. 2001; Smets and Wouters 2007; Adjemian et al. 2007).

These developments are surprising for several reasons. First, while macroeconomic theory enthusiastically embraced the view that agents fully understand the structure of the underlying models in which they operate, other sciences like psychology and neurology increasingly uncovered the cognitive limitations of individuals (see, for example, Damasio 2003; Kahneman 2002; Camerer et al. 2005). We learn from these sciences that agents understand only small bits and pieces of the world in which they live, and instead of maximizing continually taking all available information into account, agents use simple rules (heuristics) in guiding their behavior and their forecasts about the future. This raises the question of whether the micro-founded macroeconomic theory that has become the standard is well grounded scientifically.

A second source of surprise in the development of macroeconomic modeling in general and the DSGE models in particular is that other branches of economics, like game theory and experimental economics, have increasingly recognized the need to incorporate the limitations agents face in understanding the world. This has led to models that depart from the rational expectations paradigm (see, for example, Thaler 1994).

Standard macroeconomics has been immune for these developments. True, under the impulse of Sargent (1993) and Evans and Honkapohja (2001) there has been an attempt to introduce the notion in macroeconomic models that agents should not be assumed to be cleverer than econometricians and that therefore they should be modeled as agents who learn about the underlying model as time passes. This has led to learning in macroeconomics. The incorporation of learning in macroeconomics, however, has up to now left few traces in standard macroeconomic models and in the DSGE models.

Plausibility and Empirical Validity of Rational Expectations

The new Keynesian DSGE models embody the two central tenets of modern macroeconomics. The first one is that a macroeconomic model should be based ("microfounded") on dynamic utility maximization of a representative agent. The second one is that expectations should be model-consistent, which implies that agents make forecasts based on the information embedded in the model. This idea in turn implies that agents have a full understanding of the structure of the underlying model.

There can be no doubt that this approach to macroeconomics has important advantages compared with previous macroeconomic models. The main advantage is that it provides for a coherent and self-contained framework of analysis. This has great intellectual appeal. There is no need to invoke ad hoc assumptions about how agents behave and how they make forecasts. Rational expectations and utility maximization introduce discipline in modeling the behavior of agents.

The scientific validity of a model should not be based on its logical coherence or on its intellectual appeal, however. It can be judged only on its capacity to make empirical predictions that are not rejected by the data. If it fails to do so, even coherent and intellectually appealing models should be discarded. Before turning our attention to the empirical validation of models based on dynamic utility maximization and rational expectations, of which the DSGE models are now the most prominent examples, we analyze the plausibility of the underlying assumptions about human behavior in these models.

There is a very large literature documenting deviations from the paradigm of the utility-maximizing agent who understands the nature of the underlying economic model. For surveys, see Kahneman and Thaler (2006) and Della Vigna (2007). This literature has followed two tracks. One was to question the idea of utility maximization as a description of agents' behavior (see Kirchgässner (2008) for an analysis of how this idea has influenced social sciences). Many deviations have been found. A well-known one is the framing effect. Agents are often influenced by the way a choice is framed in making their decisions (see Tversky and Kahneman 1981). Another well-known deviation from the standard model is the fact that agents do not appear to attach the same utility value to gains and losses. This led Kahneman and Tversky (1973) to formulate prospect theory as an alternative to the standard utility maximization under uncertainty.

We will not deal with deviations from the standard utility-maximization model here, mainly because many (but not all) of these anomalies can be taken care of by suitably specifying alternative utility functions. Instead, we focus on the plausibility of the rational expectations assumption and its logical implication, i.e., that agents understand the nature of the underlying model.

It is no exaggeration to say that there is now overwhelming evidence that individual agents suffer from deep cognitive problems limiting their capacity to understand and to process the complexity of the information they receive.

Many anomalies that challenge the rational expectations assumption were discovered (see Thaler (1994) for spirited discussions of these anomalies; see also Camerer and Lovallo 1999; Della Vigna 2007). We just mention *anchoring effects* here, whereby agents who do not fully understand the world in which they live are highly selective in the way they use information and concentrate on the information they understand or the information that is fresh in their minds. This anchoring effect explains why agents often extrapolate recent movements in prices.

In general the cognitive problems which agents face leads them to use simple rules (*heuristics*) to guide their behavior (see Gabaix et al. 2006). They do this not because they are irrational, but rather because the complexity of the world is overwhelming. In a way it can be said that using heuristics is a rational response of agents who are aware of their limited capacity to understand the world. The challenge when we try to model heuristics is to introduce discipline in the selection of rules so as to avoid that "everything becomes possible."

One important implication of the assumption that agents know the underlying model's structure is that all agents are the same. They all use the same information set including the information embedded in the underlying model. As a result, DSGE models routinely restrict the analysis to a representative agent to fully describe how all agents in the model process information. There is no heterogeneity in the use and the processing of information in these models. This strips models based on rational expectations from much of their interest in analyzing short-term and medium-term macroeconomic problems which is about the dynamics of aggregating heterogeneous behavior and beliefs (see Solow 2005; Colander et al. 2008).[13]

It is fair to conclude that the accumulated scientific evidence casts doubts about the plausibility of the main assumption concerning the behavior of individual agents in DSGE models, i.e., that they are capable of understanding the economic model in which they operate and of processing the complex information distilled from this model. Instead, the scientific evidence suggests that individual agents are not capable of doing so, and that they rely on rules that use only small parts of the available information.

---

[13] There have been attempts to model heterogeneity of information processing in rational expectations models. These have been developed mainly in asset market models. Typically, it is assumed in these models that some agents are fully informed (rational) while others, the noise traders, are not (see, for example, De Long et al. 1990).

One could object here and argue that a model should not be judged by the plausibility of its assumptions but rather by its ability to make powerful empirical predictions. Thus, despite the apparent implausibility of its informational assumption, the macroeconomic model based on rational expectations could still be a powerful one if it makes the right predictions. This argument, which was often stressed by Milton Friedman, is entirely correct. It leads to the question of the empirical validity of the rational macromodels in general and the DSGE models in particular.

In this chapter we have discussed the failure of the DSGE models to predict a dynamics that comes close to the dynamics of the observed output movements, except when the step is taken to assume that the unexplained dynamics in the error terms is in fact an exogenous force driving an otherwise correct model. This problem of standard DSGE models has also been noted by Chari et al. (2009), who conclude that most of the dynamics produced by the standard DSGE model (e.g., Smets and Wouters 2003) comes from the autoregressive error terms, i.e., from outside the model.

The correct conclusion from such an empirical failure should be to question the underlying assumptions of the model. But surprisingly, this has not been done by DSGE modelers, who have kept their faith in the existence of rational and fully informed agents.

The issue then is how much is left over from the paradigm of the fully informed rational agent in the existing DSGE models? This leads to the question of whether it is not preferable to admit that agents' behavior is guided by heuristics, and to incorporate these heuristics into the model from the start, rather than to pretend that agents are fully rational but to rely in a nontransparent way on statistical tricks to improve the fit of the model.

Top-Down versus Bottom-Up Models

In order to understand the nature of different macroeconomic models it is useful to make a distinction between top-down and bottom-up systems. In its most general definition a top-down system is one in which one or more agents fully understand the system. These agents are capable of representing the whole system in a blueprint that they can store in their mind. Depending on their position in the system they can use this blueprint to take over the command, or they can use it to optimize their own private welfare. These are systems in which there is a one-to-one mapping of the information embedded in the system and the information contained in the brain of one (or more) individuals. An example of such a top-down system is a building that can be represented by a blueprint and is fully understood by the architect.

Bottom-up systems are very different in nature. These are systems in which no individual understands the whole picture. Each individual understands only a very small part of the whole. These systems function as a result of the application of simple rules by the individuals populating the system. Most living systems follow this bottom-up logic (see the beautiful description of the growth of the embryo by Dawkins (2009)). The market system is also a bottom-up system. The best description made of this bottom-up system is still the one made by Hayek (1945). Hayek argued that no individual exists who is capable of understanding the full complexity of a market system. Instead, individuals only understand small bits of the total information. The main function of markets consists in aggregating this diverse information. If there were individuals capable of understanding the whole picture, we would not need markets. This was in fact Hayek's criticism of the "socialist" economists who took the view that the central planner understood the whole picture, and would therefore be able to compute the whole set of optimal prices, making the market system superfluous. (For further insightful analysis see Leijonhufvud (1993).)

The previous discussion leads to the following interesting and surprising insight. Macroeconomic models that use the rational expectations assumption are the intellectual heirs of these central-planning models. Not in the sense that individuals in these rational expectations models aim at planning the whole, but in the sense that, as the central planner, they understand the whole picture. Individuals in these rational expectations models are assumed to know and understand the complex structure of the economy and the statistical distribution of all the shocks that will hit the economy. These individuals then use this superior information to obtain the "optimum optimorum" for their own private welfare. In this sense they are top-down models.

2

The Transmission of Shocks

2.1 Introduction

The economy is continually subjected to shocks. It is therefore important to find out how these shocks are transmitted into the economy. We argued in the previous chapter that in the mainstream rational expectations macroeconomic models only external shocks matter to explain movements in output and inflation. In our behavioral model there is an important endogenously generated dynamics explaining movements of output and inflation. In this chapter we analyze how this endogenous dynamics affects the transmission process of these exogenous disturbances. Different shocks will be analyzed. First we will focus on productivity shocks; second on interest rate shocks; and third on fiscal policy shocks.

2.2 The Transmission of a Positive Productivity Shock

The way we analyze how a shock is transmitted into the economy is to compute the impulse response functions. These describe the path of one of the endogenous variables (output gap, inflation) following the occurrence of the shock. In order to do so we simulate two series of these endogenous variables. One is the series without the shock (the baseline series); the other is the series with the shock. We then subtract the first from the second. This yields a new series, the impulse response that shows how the endogenous variable that embodies the shock evolves relative to the benchmark. These impulse responses are expressed as "multipliers," i.e., the output and inflation responses to the shock are divided by the shock itself (which is one standard deviation of the error term in the supply equation).

The behavioral model is nonlinear. Therefore, during the post-shock period we continue to allow for random disturbances. Thus the impulse response measures the response to the exogenous shock in an environment in which the random disturbances are the same for the series with and without the shock.

The exercise was repeated 500 times with 500 different realizations of the random disturbances. The mean impulse response together with the standard deviation were then computed. We define the productivity shock to be a one standard deviation shock of the random disturbances of the aggregate supply equation. The results are

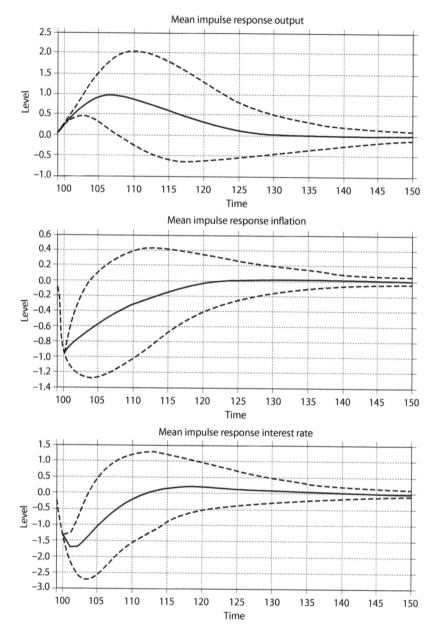

Figure 2.1.   Mean impulse responses of output gap, inflation, and interest rate to positive productivity shock.

shown in figure 2.1, which shows the mean response (full line) and ±2 standard deviations away from the mean (dashed lines). Note also that we introduced the shock after 100 periods.

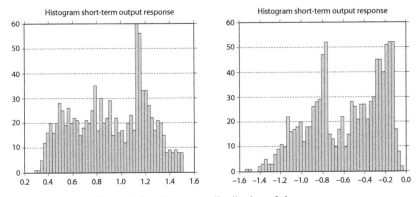

Figure 2.2. Frequency distribution of short-term
output gap and inflation effect of productivity shock.

From figure 2.1 several conclusions can be derived. First, the positive productivity shock has the expected macroeconomic effects. In the short term the output gap increases and inflation declines. In addition, the interest rate declines. This is so because the central bank follows a Taylor rule in which the weight attached to inflation is much higher than the weight attached to the output gap (the coefficient of inflation is 1.5 while the coefficient of the output gap is 0.5). As a result the decline in inflation leads the central bank to lower the interest rate so as to bring inflation back to its target. Second, in the long run these effects tend to disappear. Note, however, that the level of output is permanently higher in the long-run equilibrium (because the productivity shock has raised capacity output).

Third, and most importantly, there is a wide variation in the short-term effects of the productivity shock. This can be seen from the fact that dotted lines representing ±2 standard deviations from the mean are very far from the mean. Thus it is very difficult to predict how the same productivity shock affects the output gap and inflation in the short run. This uncertainty can also be illustrated by presenting the frequency distribution of the short-term output gap and inflation effects of the productivity shock. We show these in figure 2.2. We define the short term as six periods (approximately half a year). The divergence in the effects of the same productivity shock is striking. It ranges from +0.4% to 1.6% for the output gap and from −0.1 to almost −1.5% for inflation. We also note that the statistical distribution of these short-term effects is far from the normal distribution and exhibits fat tails. Thus the same productivity shock can lead to strong outlying effects. The nonnormal distribution of the short-term effects adds to the unpredictability of these effects. Thus, the transmission of the shock is shrouded by the veil of uncertainty (in the sense of Frank Knight).

Where does this uncertainty come from? Not from parameter uncertainty. The same parameters are used in constructing all our impulse responses. The answer is that in this behavioral model each realization of the shocks creates different waves

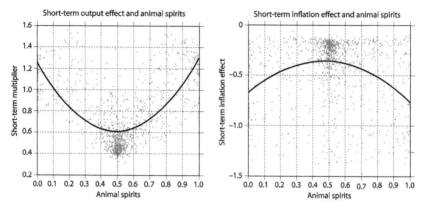

Figure 2.3.   Effects of productivity shock depend on market sentiments.

of optimism and pessimism (animal spirits). One could also call these "market sentiments." Thus a shock that occurs in one simulation happens in a different market sentiment than the same shock in another simulation. In addition, the shock itself affects market sentiments. As a result, the short-term effects of the same productivity shock become very hard to predict.

We show the importance of these market sentiments in figure 2.3. On the horizontal axis we plot the mean value of the animal spirits index up to the sixth period after the productivity shock (remember that we defined the short-term effect to be the effect six periods after the shock). On the vertical axis the short-term output and inflation effects (respectively) are shown. Thus these figures show the relation between market sentiments prevailing during the adjustment period following the shock (including the period of the shock) and the size of the short-term effect of the productivity shock. The most striking aspect of this relation is that animal spirits matter a great deal for the intensity of the effects of a productivity shock. This is very clear from the left-hand panel (representing the output effect); less so from the right-hand panel (representing the inflation effect). We observe that when there are no strong optimistic or pessimistic market sentiments, the short-term output effect is on average 0.6; when the market has turned into extreme optimism or pessimism the same productivity shock has a short-term output effect that is about twice as high on average, i.e., 1.2. Thus it appears that animal spirits amplify the short-term effects of a given productivity shock. When optimism prevails, a positive productivity shock creates a much stronger boom in the economy than in a neutral state of market sentiments (animal spirits index = 0.5). Similarly, when pessimism prevails the positive productivity shock has a strong positive output effect because it quickly ends the period of pessimism.

Note, however, that the variance around the fitted curves is very large. Thus although market sentiments matter, there remains a lot of uncertainty about its effect in the transmission process.

The results of the transmission of a productivity shock in a behavioral model contrast a great deal with the results obtained in the mainstream rational expectations model. In the latter model there is no uncertainty about the transmission of a productivity shock. If we know the parameters of the model we can calculate the impulse response function with exact precision. It does not depend at all on the precise timing of the shock. The only uncertainty comes from the uncertainty about the parameters of the model. But this uncertainty also exists in a behavioral model. Thus, the mainstream rational expectations model creates the illusion of excessive precision. If we have a lot of precise knowledge about the parameters of the model, we also have a lot of precision about the transmission of an exogenous shock. But this may not be the case if as in our behavioral model the existence of animal spirits (market sentiments) creates great uncertainty about this transmission.

2.3 The Transmission of Interest Rate Shocks

In this section we focus on the question of how an interest rate shock is transmitted in the economy. We use the same techniques as in the previous section, i.e., we compute the impulse responses to a positive interest rate shock, defined as an increase in the interest rate equal to one standard deviation of the random disturbances in the Taylor equation. We show the results in figures 2.4 and 2.5.

The impulse response functions (figure 2.4) and the frequency distributions of the short-term effects (figure 2.5) were computed in the same way as in the previous section. We concentrate on the impulse response functions first. We find the traditional result (obtained in mainstream models) concerning the effects of an increase in the interest rate. The output gap and the rate of inflation decline following the increase in the interest rate. The decline in output, however, is swifter and more intense than the decline in the rate of inflation. This has to do with the built-in wage and price rigidities in the model.

As in the previous section we find considerable uncertainty about the short-term transmission of the interest rate increase. This can be seen both from the wide band of uncertainty around the mean impulse response in figure 2.4 and the frequency distribution of the short-term effects (figure 2.5). The latter are not normally distributed and exhibit fat tails. The irregular nature of these frequency distributions (despite the fact that we performed 1000 different calculations of impulse responses) suggests that it will be very difficult to make precise probabilistic statements about the short-term output and inflation effects of an interest rate shock.

As before this uncertainty does not come from parameter uncertainty. The same parameters are used in constructing all our impulse responses. The uncertainty comes from the fact that, in this behavioral model, each realization of the shocks creates different waves of optimism and pessimism (animal spirits) that affect the transmission of the interest rate shock. This kind of uncertainty is absent from mainstream rational expectations models. In these models we know the transmission

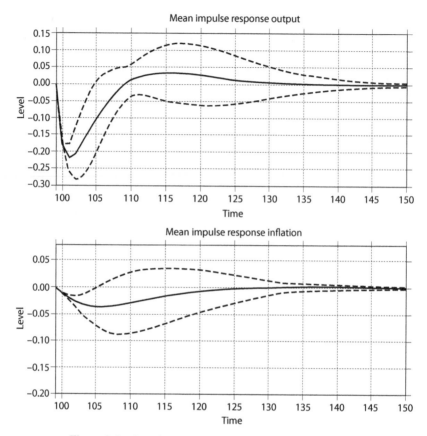

Figure 2.4.   Impulse response to positive interest rate shock.

of monetary policy with precision if the parameters of the model are known with precision.

The behavioral model contrasts with the mainstream new Keynesian rational expectations model in that in the former the timing of the shock matters. The same shocks applied at different times can have very different short-term effects on inflation and output. In other words, history matters. This is not the case in the mainstream model: the same interest rate shock always has the same effect whatever the timing of the shock.

Note that the uncertainty about the impulse responses tends to disappear in the long run, as the effect of short-term differences in market sentiments disappears.

Finally, we also analyzed the question of how the transmission of the interest rate shock is influenced by the market sentiments (animal spirits). We use the same procedure as in the previous section. This yields figure 2.6. On the horizontal axis the animal spirits index is shown. As before, it varies between 0 and 1. When the index is 0 all agents are extrapolating a negative output gap, i.e., pessimism is at

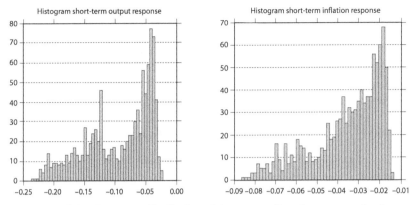

Figure 2.5. Frequency distribution of short-term effects interest rate shock.

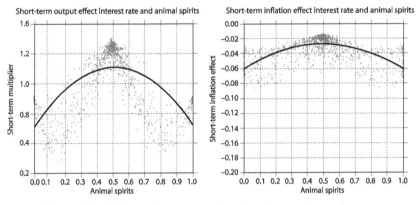

Figure 2.6. Effects of monetary policy depend on market sentiments.

the highest level. When the index is 1 all agents extrapolate a positive output gap. Optimism is at its peak. When the index is equal to 0.5 few agents are in fact extrapolating, and most are following a fundamentalist rule, i.e., they expect the output gap to return to 0 (its steady-state value). On the vertical axes of figure 2.6 the short-term output effect and the short-term inflation effect (respectively) of an interest rate increase are shown.

The results of figure 2.6 lend themselves to the following interpretation. First, animal spirits have a strong impact on the short-term output effect of the same interest rate shock. In general, the stronger the animal spirits, i.e., the stronger optimism and pessimism are, the greater is the short-term impact of the interest rate shock on output. In contrast, when animal spirits are weak (the index is close to 0.5) the impact is weakest. Thus, when the market is dominated by either optimism or pessimism, the monetary authorities' interest rate instrument has the greatest impact on output (in the short run). Like in the case of a productivity shock animal spirits tend to amplify the short-term effects of monetary policies. These effects, however, tend to disappear in the long run.

Second, the animal spirits have a much lower impact on the effectiveness of monetary policy to move inflation. This is made clear from contrasting the two graphs in figure 2.6, which shows a low sensitivity of animal spirits on the impact of an interest rate shock on inflation.

2.4   Fiscal Policy Multipliers: How Much Do We Know?

Since the eruption of the financial crisis in 2007–8 governments of major countries have applied massive policies of fiscal stimulus. This has led to a heated debate about the size of the fiscal policy multipliers. This debate has revealed (once more) how divergent economists' views are about the size of these multipliers (see Wieland et al. 2009). The estimates of the short-term multipliers vary from 0 to numbers far exceeding 1. There has been a lot of soul searching about the reasons for these widely divergent estimates.

An important source of these differences is to be found in the use of different models that embody different priors. For example, in mainstream macroeconomic models that incorporate agents with rational expectations (both new classical and the new Keynesian) fiscal policy multipliers are likely to be very small, as these models typically have Ricardian equivalence embedded in the model, i.e., agents anticipating future tax increases following a fiscal stimulus (budget deficit) will start saving more (consuming less) so that one dollar of government spending is offset by 1 dollar less of private spending. In these models the fiscal policy multiplier is close to 0. In Keynesian models there is scope for a net stimulatory effect of fiscal policies. Thus, the different estimates of fiscal policy multipliers are not "neutral estimates" but reflect theoretical priors and beliefs that have been put in these models in the construction stage.

Our behavioral model allows us to shed some additional light on the uncertainty surrounding the effects of fiscal policies. We will do this by studying how a positive shock in aggregate demand produced by a fiscal expansion affects output. We will not give an exhaustive analysis of fiscal policies. Our model does not incorporate the detail of government spending and taxation to be able to do this. In particular, it sidesteps the issue of how the additional government spending is financed, i.e., by debt issue of taxation.[1] We model a fiscal policy shock just as a shock in the demand equation. What the model allows us to establish is the nature of uncertainty surrounding such a shock even in an extremely simple model, i.e., one that disregards all the issues relating to the way such government spending is financed.

We assume the fiscal policy expansion to occur under two different monetary policy regimes. In the first regime we assume that the central bank uses the standard

---

[1] For such a model, see example, Blanchard and Fischer (1989) and Romer (2005).

Taylor rule as specified in equation (1.3). Thus under this regime the fiscal policy expansion will automatically lead the central bank to raise the interest rate. This follows from the fact that the demand stimulus produces an increase in output and inflation to which the central bank reacts by raising the interest rate.

In the second regime we assume that the central bank does not react to the stimulus-induced expansion of output and inflation by raising the interest rate. We do this, not because it is realistic, but rather to estimate the pure Keynesian multiplier effect of a fiscal stimulus. The Keynesian multiplier is usually estimated under the assumption of a constant interest rate so that crowding out does not occur. Note that this is also the multiplier that is obtained when the economy is in a liquidity trap.

We show the results of this fiscal policy stimulus under the two monetary policy regimes in figure 2.7. The upper two panels show the impulse responses under the two monetary policy regimes. The instantaneous effects of the fiscal stimulus are the same under the two regimes. However, under the variable interest rate regime the positive effects of the fiscal stimulus decline much faster and undershoot in the negative region more than under the constant interest regime. This is not surprising, since under the variable interest rate regime we see that the interest rate is raised quite substantially (see bottom panel), leading to a quick crowding out.

A second important difference concerns the degree of uncertainty about the size of the output effects of a fiscal stimulus. As the upper panels show the divergences of the impulse responses are much larger in the constant interest rate regime than in the variable interest rate regime. This is also illustrated in the second set of panels. These show the frequency distribution of the short-term output responses under the two regimes. We observe a much wider spread of these short-term output responses under the fixed interest rate regime. The reason is found in the third set of panels. These show that the short-term output responses are more sensitive to animal spirits in the fixed interest rate regime than in the variable one. Thus the interest rate response under the variable interest rate regime tends to reduce the impact of animal spirits on the transmission mechanism, thereby reducing the volatility in this transmission. Put differently, when as a result of the fiscal expansion the central bank raises the interest rate, it lowers the expansionary effect of this expansion, making it less likely that positive animal spirits will enhance the fiscal policy stimulus.

These results make clear that there is likely to be a great amount of uncertainty about the size of the output effects of fiscal policies. This uncertainty is even more pronounced in the Keynesian scenario of constant interest rate. This is also the scenario usually associated with the occurrence of a liquidity trap (a horizontal LM-curve). This is the assumption that tends to make fiscal policies most effective. In our model it is also the assumption making the uncertainty about the size of these effects the greatest.

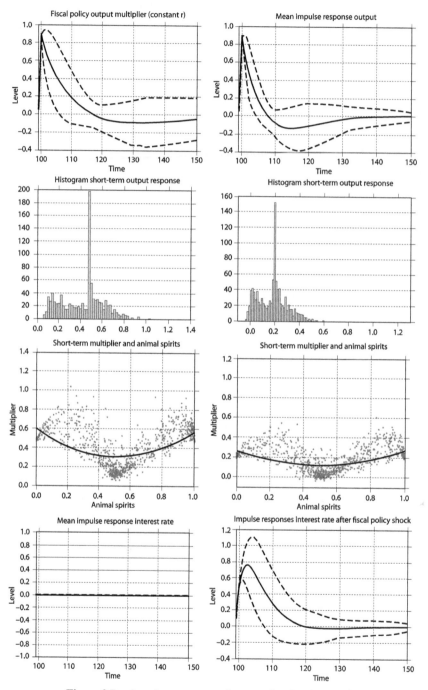

Figure 2.7.   Impulse responses of output after fiscal expansion.

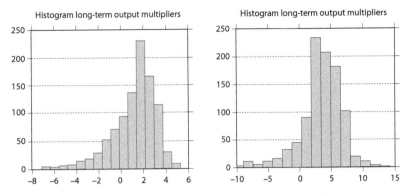

Figure 2.8. Long-term fiscal policy multipliers: frequency distribution.

These differences are also made clear from a comparison of the long-term fiscal policy multipliers obtained from the same simulations as in figure 2.7. The fiscal policy shock underlying the previous simulations is a one-period increase in demand (by one standard deviation). (The closest example of such a shock is the Cash for Clunkers car-buying stimulus programs introduced in many European countries and in the United States in 2009 to fight the recession.) This temporary increase then produces the impulse responses as given in figure 2.7. In order to obtain the long-term multipliers we add up all the output increases (and declines) following this temporary fiscal policy shock. We show these long-term fiscal policy multipliers in figure 2.8 under the two monetary policy regimes.

Two results stand out. First, as expected, the long-term fiscal policy multipliers are much higher under the constant interest rate rule than under the variable interest rate rule. Second, the uncertainty surrounding these long-term multipliers is considerable. And this uncertainty is the most pronounced under the constant interest rate rule.

It should be stressed again that the nature of the uncertainty here is not the uncertainty surrounding the parameters of the model. We assume exactly the same parameters in all these simulations. Put differently, it is not the uncertainty produced by the use of different models with different prior beliefs about the effectiveness of fiscal policies that produce uncertainty. The uncertainty is due to differences in initial conditions (market sentiments). These differences in market sentiments have a pronounced effect on how the same fiscal policy shock is transmitted in the economy.

2.5 Transmission under Perfect Credibility of Inflation Target

In the previous chapter we found that the occurrence of animal spirits also depends on the monetary regime. In particular, we found that when the inflation targeting regime is perfectly credible, the power of animal spirits to shape the business

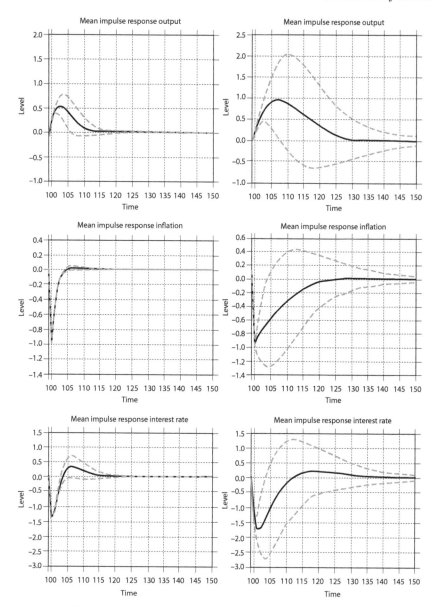

Figure 2.9.   Impulse responses to a positive productivity shock.

cycle is greatly diminished. This raises the question of whether a perfectly credible inflation-targeting regime may not also greatly affect the transmission of shocks.

We analyze this question by computing the impulse responses to exogenous shocks under the assumption that perfect credibility of inflation targeting prevails. The procedure is the same as in the previous section. We first show the impulse responses to a positive productivity shock. The results are shown in figure 2.9. The contrast with the impulse responses obtained under imperfect credibility (which are the same impulse responses as in figure 2.1) is striking. We find three important differences. First the short-term impact of the productivity shock on output is greatly reduced in a regime of perfect credibility. This has to do with the fact that in the absence of animal spirits the amplification effect of exogenous shocks disappears. Second, under perfect credibility the time it takes for the endogenous variables (output gap, inflation, interest rate) to return to their long-term values is much shorter than under imperfect credibility. Third, under perfect credibility, the uncertainty surrounding the short-term effects of the exogenous shocks is greatly reduced. From figure 2.9 we observe that the impulse response path is much more precise (much lower standard deviations) in the perfect credibility regime than in the imperfect credibility one. As a result, in an environment of perfectly credible inflation targeting the effects of an exogenous shock can be predicted with much greater precision than in a regime of imperfectly credible inflation targeting. In such a monetary regime the Knightian uncertainty is much less prevalent and we return to the world of quantifiable risk.

3
Trade-offs between Output and Inflation Variability

3.1 Introduction

Modern macroeconomics in general and DSGE models in particular have provided the intellectual foundation of inflation targeting. Until the eruption of the financial crisis in 2007, inflation targeting strategies had become the undisputed policy framework modern central banks should adopt. And most did. The official holders of macroeconomic wisdom declared that this step towards inflation targeting constituted a great victory of macroeconomics as a science (Woodford 2009). From now on we would be living in a more stable macroeconomic environment, a "Great Moderation." How things can change so quickly.

Inflation targeting, of course, does not imply that there is no role for output stabilization. New Keynesian DSGE modelers have always stressed that wage and price rigidities provide a rationale for output stabilization by central banks (see Clarida et al. 1999; Galí 2008). This idea has found its reflection in "flexible" inflation targeting (Svensson 1997; Woodford 2003). Because of the existence of rigidities, a central bank should not attempt to keep inflation close to its target all the time. When sufficiently large shocks occur that lead to departures of inflation from its target, the central bank should follow a strategy of gradual return of inflation to its target. The rationale is that in a world of wage and price rigidities too abrupt attempts to bring inflation back to its target would require such high increases in the interest rate as to produce overly strong declines in output.

Output stabilization in the DSGE world, however, is very much circumscribed. The need to stabilize output arises because of the existence of rigidities in prices that makes it necessary to spread out price movements over longer periods. The limited scope for output stabilization is based on a model characterized by a stable equilibrium. There is no consideration of the possibility that the equilibrium may be unstable or that fluctuations in output have a different origin than price rigidities. Should the scope for output stabilization be enlarged? This is the question we try to answer in this chapter. In order to shed some light on this issue we derive the trade-off between output and inflation variability in the context of our behavioral model, and we formulate some policy conclusions.

3.2 Constructing Trade-offs

The trade-offs between output and inflation variability are constructed in the following way. The model was simulated 10,000 times and the average output and inflation variability were computed for different values of the Taylor rule parameters. Figure 3.1 shows how output variability (panel (a)) and inflation variability (panel (b)) change as the output coefficient (c_2) in the Taylor rule increases from 0 to 1. Each line represents the outcome for different values of the inflation coefficient (c_1) in the Taylor rule.

Panel (a) showing the evolution of output variability exhibits the expected result, i.e., as the output coefficient (c_2) increases (i.e., inflation targeting becomes less strict) output variability tends to decrease. One would now expect that this decline in output variability resulting from more active stabilization comes at the cost of more inflation variability. This is what is generally found in mainstream new Keynesian rational expectations models (see Galí 2008). This, however, is not found in panel (b). One observes that the relationship is nonlinear. As the output coefficient is increased from 0, inflation variability first declines. Only when the output coefficient increases beyond a certain value (in a range 0.6–0.8) inflation variability starts increasing. Thus the central bank can reduce both output *and* inflation variability when it moves away from strict inflation targeting ($c_2 = 0$) and engages in some output stabilization. Not too much though. Too much output stabilization turns around the relationship and increases inflation variability.

Figure 3.1 allows us to construct the trade-offs between output and inflation variability. These are shown in figure 3.2 for different values of the inflation parameter c_1. Take the trade-off AB. This is the one obtained for $c_1 = 1$. Start from point A on the trade-off. At point A, the output parameter $c_2 = 0$ (strict inflation targeting). As output stabilization increases we first move downwards. Thus increased output stabilization by the central bank reduces output and inflation variability. The relation is nonlinear, however. At some point, with too high an output stabilization parameter, the trade-off curve starts increasing, becoming a "normal" trade-off, i.e., a lower output variability is obtained at the cost of increased inflation variability.

How can we interpret these results? Let us start from the case of strict inflation targeting, i.e., the authorities set $c_2 = 0$. There is no attempt at stabilizing output at all. The ensuing output variability intensifies the waves of optimism and pessimism (animal spirits), which in turn feed back on output volatility. These large waves lead to higher inflation variability. Thus, some output stabilization is good; it reduces both output and inflation variability by preventing too large swings in animal spirits. With no output stabilization at all ($c_2 = 0$) the forces of animal spirits are so high that the high output variability also increases inflation volatility through the effect of the output gap on inflation (supply equation). Too much output stabilization, however, reduces the stabilization bonus provided by a credible inflation target. When the

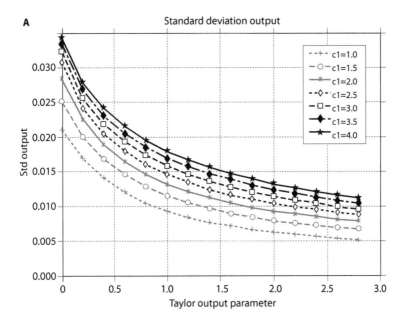

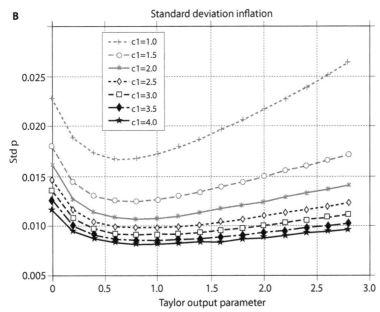

Figure 3.1. Output and inflation variability.

central bank attaches too much importance to output stabilization, it creates more
scope for better forecasting performance of the inflation extrapolators, leading to
more inflation variability.

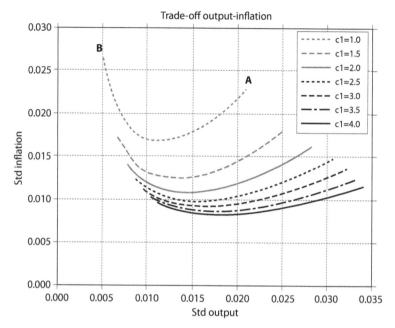

Figure 3.2. Trade-offs in the behavioral model.

Figure 3.2 also tells us something important about inflation targeting. We note that increasing the inflation parameter in the Taylor rule (c_1) has the effect of shifting the trade-offs downwards, i.e., the central bank can improve the trade-offs by reacting more strongly to changes in inflation.[1] The central bank achieves this improvement in the trade-off because by reacting more intensely to changes in inflation it reduces the probability that inflation extrapolators will tend to dominate the market, and as a result it reduces the probability that inflation targeting loses credibility. Such a loss of credibility destabilizes both inflation and output. Thus maintaining credibility of inflation targeting is an important source of macroeconomic stability in our behavioral model.

Note that the downward movements of the trade-offs tend to slow down with increasing values of the inflation parameter in the Taylor rule (c_1). Additional simulations show that when c_1 reaches the value of 6, further increases in this parameter have imperceptible effects on the trade-offs. In other words, the trade-offs converge to a stable position. The minimum point on this trade-off then represents the best possible outcome for a central bank, which focuses on minimizing the variability of inflation. It is the best possible point for a central bank that only cares

---

[1] A similar result on the importance of strict inflation is found in Gaspar et al. (2006), who use a macromodel with statistical learning. See also Anufriev et al. (2009) for the use of interest rate rules in a model with heterogeneous agents.

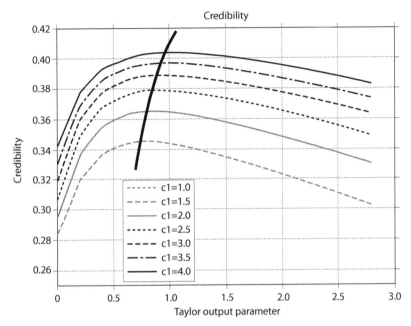

Figure 3.3. Inflation credibility and output stabilization.

about inflation. The interesting implication is that the central bank can only achieve this point if it actively tries to stabilize output.

The previous results suggest that there is a relationship between the parameters c_1 and c_2 in the Taylor equation and the credibility of the inflation target. This relationship can be analyzed in more detail. Inflation credibility can be given a precise definition in the model. It can be defined as the fraction of agents who use the inflation target to forecast inflation ("inflation targeters"). Thus when more agents use the announced inflation target to forecast inflation, credibility increases. Figure 3.3 presents the relationship between inflation credibility and the parameters c_1 and c_2. On the horizontal axis the parameter c_2 (output parameter) is set out; on the vertical axis the inflation credibility. The latter is obtained by simulating the model 10,000 times and computing the mean fractions of inflation targeters for different values of the c_1 and c_2. Each curve represents the relation between credibility and the output parameter (c_2) for different values of the inflation parameter (c_1). It has a nonlinear feature, i.e., when the output parameter c_2 increases this has the effect of first increasing inflation credibility until a maximum is reached. Then credibility starts declining when c_2 increases further. This nonlinear feature is found for all values of c_1. Note that the maximum points obtained in figure 3.3 correspond to the minimum point of the trade-offs in figure 3.2.

These results have the following interpretation. When the central bank increases its effort to stabilize output, this has at first a positive effect on the credibility

Table 3.1. Pairwise Granger causality tests.

Null hypothesis	Obs.	F-Statistic	Probability
Output does not Granger cause optimism	1948	31.0990	5.1E-14
Optimism does not Granger cause output		32.8553	9.3E-15

of its inflation target.[2] The reason, as was discussed earlier, is that by stabilizing output, the central bank also reduces the amplitude of the waves of optimism and pessimism (animal spirits) thereby stabilizing output and inflation. Inflation credibility is maximized when c_2 is in a range between 0.5 and 1. Beyond that range further attempts to stabilize output reduce inflation credibility for the reasons given earlier. The interesting aspect of this result is that the optimal values of c_2 are in a range often found in econometric studies of the Taylor equation. Thus central banks seem to apply a degree of output stabilization that is consistent with our theory of animal spirits.

Finally, figure 3.3 shows that for increasing values of c_1 the credibility curves shift upwards. Thus a central bank can improve its inflation credibility by reacting more strongly to changes in inflation. This feature then underlies the result found in figure 3.2 that higher values of c_1 improve the trade-off between inflation and output variability.

One can conclude that the behavioral model provides a different perspective on the need to stabilize output. This is a model that creates endogenous movements of the business cycle that are correlated with waves of optimism and pessimism. These waves of optimism and pessimism both influence the output gap and in turn are also influenced by the output gap. We show this two-way causality feature in Table 3.1, where the results of a Granger causality test on the output gap and the animal spirits (as defined in chapter 1) are presented. It can be seen that one cannot reject the hypotheses that animal spirits "Granger cause" the output gap and that the output gap "Granger causes" the animal spirits.

This two-way causality between output gap and animal spirits creates the possibility for the central bank to reduce the waves of optimism and pessimism by reducing the volatility of output. In doing so, the central bank creates a more stable macroeconomic environment that also helps to stabilize inflation.

3.3　Trade-offs in the New Keynesian Rational Expectations (DSGE) Model

The trade-offs in the new Keynesian rational expectations (DSGE) model can be computed in a way similar to that of the previous section. Thus we constructed the trade-offs using the rational expectations version of the basic model (see equations

---

[2] For an interesting analysis of credibility issues in a model with less than full rational expectations, see Ball et al. (2005).

(1.25) and (1.26)).[3] The trade-offs are represented in figure 3.4. The difference with figure 3.2 is striking. First, in the DSGE rational expectations world, trade-offs are uniformly downward sloping. This means that when the central bank increases the intensity with which it stabilizes output it always pays a price, i.e., success in reducing the variability of output is paid by a higher variability of inflation. This implies that if the central bank attaches a high weight to the inflation target it will usually not pay off to try to stabilize output (see Galí 2008, p. 83; Woodford 2003). This contrasts with the result obtained in a behavioral model. There we found that a central bank that only cares about inflation would still want to do a lot of output stabilization because the latter reduces the importance of animal spirits and thus also reduces inflation volatility. That is also why in the behavioral model we find that the central bank can improve its *inflation* credibility by doing more output stabilization. This effect is absent in the mainstream rational expectations model.

A second contrast in the trade-offs of the mainstream new Keynesian rational expectations (DSGE) model and the behavioral model relates to the size of the variability of inflation and output. This is in general significantly lower in the mainstream model than in the behavioral model. Put differently, the trade-offs tend to be located closer to the origin in the mainstream model than in the behavioral model. This result is not due to the fact that the shocks are different. In both models we assume shocks in demand and supply equations that are i.i.d. and which have the same standard deviations. The reason is that the behavioral model creates more endogenous variability, which as was shown in chapter 3 is not normally distributed. This creates more scope for stabilization.

Finally, a comparison of figures 3.2 and 3.4 also reveals that the "efficient trade-off," i.e., the lowest possible trade-off, is reached with lower values of the Taylor inflation parameter in the mainstream model than in the behavioral model. We observe that for values of c_1 exceeding 1.5 very little improvement in the trade-off can be achieved by raising this parameter. In the behavioral model the value of c_1 that leads to the lowest possible trade-off is reached around 4. Thus, in the behavioral model it requires more effort from the central bank to achieve the best possible outcome.

3.4 The Merits of Strict Inflation Targeting

From the preceding analysis it has become clear that a central bank that cares about inflation should also be concerned with output stabilization. Thus, strict inflation targeting in the sense of setting the output coefficient in the Taylor equation equal to zero is never optimal. In this section we further illustrate the non-optimality of strict inflation targeting. We do this in two ways.

---

[3] As in the previous section we first compute the variability of output and inflation for different values of the output and inflation parameters in the Taylor rule equation. We then plot the variabilities of output and inflation in one quadrant (figure 3.4).

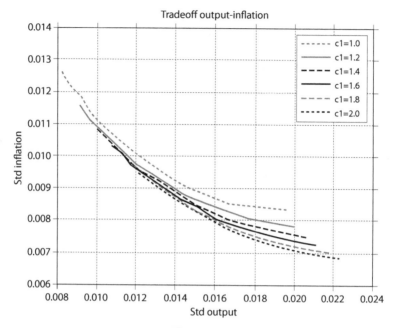

Figure 3.4.

First we simulated the model under perfect credibility and assuming that the central bank ceases to stabilize output. We achieve this by setting the output coefficient in the Taylor equation equal to zero. We will refer to this policy regime as a regime of strict inflation targeting, i.e., the central bank only cares about inflation.[4] We show the result of simulating the model under this regime in figure 3.5. Animal spirits now work with full force. In fact we find them to be stronger than in the case of imperfect credibility with output stabilization (which we discussed in chapter 1, figures 1.7 and 1.8). As a result, fat tails are pronounced leading to large extreme values for the output gap, i.e., large booms and busts. Inflation, in contrast, continues to be normally distributed.

A second way to analyze the implications of strict inflation targeting is to analyze the impulse response functions in a regime of strict inflation targeting. We do this in figure 3.6, which shows the impulse response function under the assumption that the central bank uses strict inflation targeting, i.e., sets the output coefficient in the Taylor rule equal to zero in an environment in which its inflation target is imperfectly credible.

From figure 3.6 we observe that the productivity shock introduces a cyclical transmission process. This cyclical adjustment process is not present when the central bank attempts to stabilize output (see chapter 2). In the very long run, the

---

[4] Note that in chapter 1 we also simulated the model under strict inflation targeting (figure 1.13). However, there we assumed imperfect credibility.

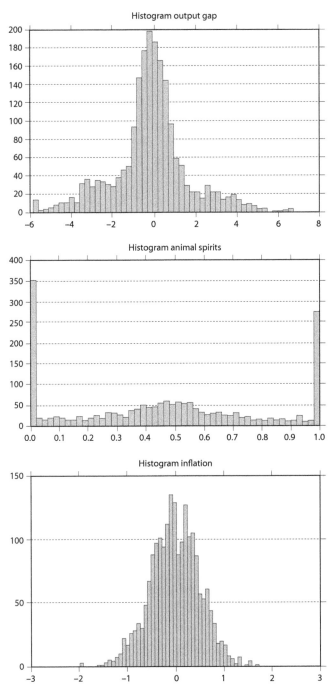

Figure 3.5. Frequency distribution output gap, animal spirits, and inflation in a regime of perfect inflation credibility and strict inflation targeting.

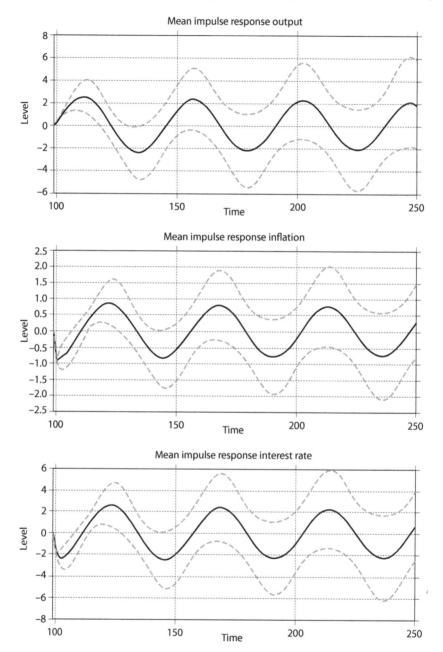

Figure 3.6. Impulse responses to positive productivity shock.

endogenous variables, output, inflation, and interest rate converge to their steady-state values, but this process is very protracted. This cyclical adjustment process is also present in inflation. Thus, by focusing exclusively on stabilizing inflation, the central bank makes the transmission of the productivity shock on inflation more volatile than in a regime where the central bank does not focus exclusively on inflation. One can conclude that strict inflation targeting is unlikely to be optimal.

As was mentioned in the beginning of the chapter, mainstream new Keynesian rational expectations models come to a similar conclusion, i.e., that strict inflation targeting is not optimal. Central banks are also responsible for some output stabilization. The need for output stabilization, however, arises exclusively because of price and wage rigidities. The latter require the central banks to apply gradualism in pursuing its inflation objective. But this always comes at a cost, i.e., more inflation variability.

We have shown that there is an additional dimension to output stabilization. By reducing output volatility, central banks also help to "tame the animal spirits." This in turn reduces the variability of inflation and helps (rather than hurts) the central bank in achieving its inflation objective.

Flexibility, Animal Spirits, and Stabilization

4.1 Introduction

Modern macroeconomics stresses the crucial importance of price flexibility. The new classical model predicts that when prices are perfectly flexible, output movements are independent of monetary policy (Woodford 2003; Galí 2008). In that case, shocks in output can only occur as a result of "real" shocks, e.g., productivity shocks, changes in preferences. It also follows that in such a world of perfect price flexibility there is no scope for output stabilization by the monetary authorities. Do these propositions also hold in our behavioral model? We answer this question in the current chapter.

4.2 Flexibility and Neutrality of Money

The way we answer this question is by reverting to the basic aggregate demand and supply model of chapter 1 (equations (1.1) and (1.2)) and to eliminate the lags in these equations. We reproduce the model consisting of an aggregate demand and supply equation here:

$$y_t = \tilde{E}_t y_{t+1} + a_2(r_t - \tilde{E}_t \pi_{t+1}) + \varepsilon_t, \tag{4.1}$$

$$\pi_t = \tilde{E}_t \pi_{t+1} + b_2 y_t + \eta_t. \tag{4.2}$$

We will now allow changes to occur in the parameter b_2. It can be shown that b_2 varies between 0 and ∞ and that these values depend on the degree of price rigidity in the context of a Calvo pricing assumption (see Galí 2008). The case of $b_2 = 0$ corresponds to complete price rigidity (firms have a zero probability of changing prices in period t) and $b_2 = \infty$ to perfect price flexibility (firms have a probability 1 of changing prices in period t). The former case can also be represented by a horizontal aggregate supply curve, while the latter is represented by a vertical aggregate supply curve. In the latter case the model can be called the new classical model of perfect flexibility of wages and prices.

We now allow the parameter b_2 to vary from 0 to 5 and we compute two indicators of the capacity of the behavioral model to generate endogenous business cycles. The first one is the autocorrelation coefficient of the output gap, and the second one

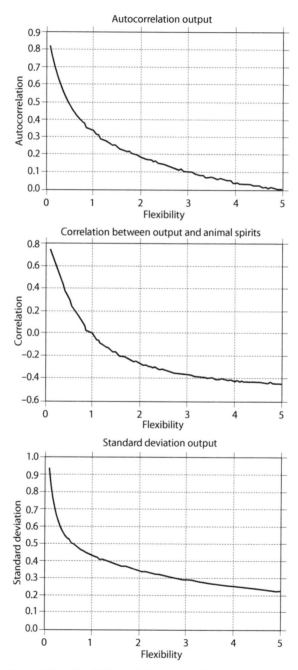

Figure 4.1. Flexibility and the nature of the business cycle.

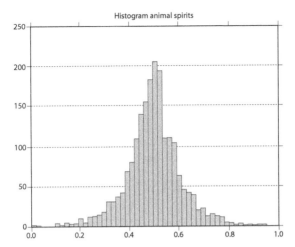

Figure 4.2. Frequency distribution of animal spirits with high flexibility.

is the correlation coefficient between the output gap and animal spirits. Remember that all shocks in the model are white noise (no autocorrelation). Thus, if the model produces autocorrelation in the output gap, this must be due to an endogenous dynamics. The second indicator tells us how much the output gap dynamics is related to animal spirits. We show the results in figure 4.1. We have also added the standard deviation of the output gap in the third panel.

Our results are quite striking. As b_2 increases (flexibility increases), the degree of autocorrelation of output declines (first panel). This decline is associated with a decline in the correlation between output and animal spirits (second panel). In fact, when $b_2 = 5$ there are no animal spirits anymore. All this contributes to less volatility of output (third panel in figure 4.1). Thus an increase in price flexibility reduces and even eliminates the occurrence of animal spirits thereby eliminating an important source of business cycle movements. It also contributes to less volatility in output.

We illustrate the disappearance of animal spirits when flexibility is sufficiently high in figure 4.2, which presents the frequency distribution of animal spirits when $b_2 = 5$. We find that there are practically no observations of extreme values of either 0 (extreme pessimism) or 1 (extreme optimism).

Flexibility contributes to less volatility of output. This comes at a price, however. When flexibility increases inflation volatility increases. This is shown in figure 4.3.

The effect of flexibility on the nature of output fluctuations can also be seen from table 4.1. This shows the correlation coefficients of output with three variables, i.e., demand shocks (ε_t in the demand equation), supply shocks (η_t in the new Keynesian Philips curve equation), and animal spirits. For low levels of flexibility we observe from table 4.1 that the movements of output are dominated by the movements of animal spirits, while the effect of exogenous demand and supply shocks on output

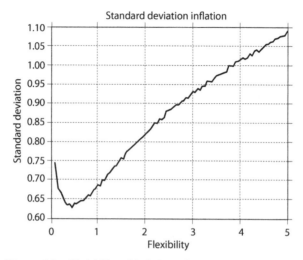

Figure 4.3.   Variability of inflation when flexibility increases.

Table 4.1.   Correlation coefficients of output gap with shocks and animal spirits.

	$b_2 = 0.05$	$b_2 = 0.5$	$b_2 = 5$
Demand shock	0.39	0.70	0.78
Supply shock	−0.08	−0.22	−0.24
Animal spirits	0.74	0.46	0.19

is relatively small. As flexibility increases the influence of exogenous shocks on output increases while the animal spirits become less important (as measured by the correlation coefficient).

How can these results be interpreted? When price flexibility is high, price changes take much of the burden in adjustment to shocks. As a result, output volatility is small. In this environment of low output volatility, animal spirits, which feed on the uncertainty about business cycle movements, find little "breeding ground." Put differently, when output does not move much, self-fulfilling waves of optimism and pessimism about future output movements do not easily emerge. They cease to be important. As a result, output movements are mainly determined by exogenous demand and supply shocks.

4.3   Flexibility and Stabilization

The drastically different macroeconomic regimes produced by flexibility also translate into very different monetary policy regimes. We illustrate these differences by presenting the impulse responses to the same interest rate shocks for four different values of b_2 (see figure 4.4). We observe that as flexibility increases the effect of an

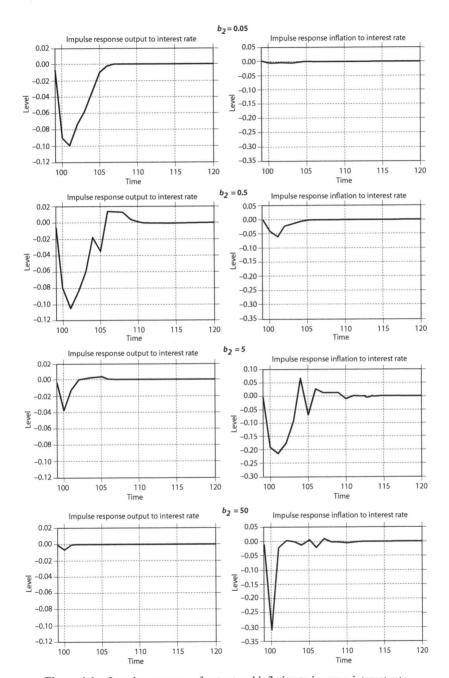

Figure 4.4. Impulse response of output and inflation to increase interest rate.

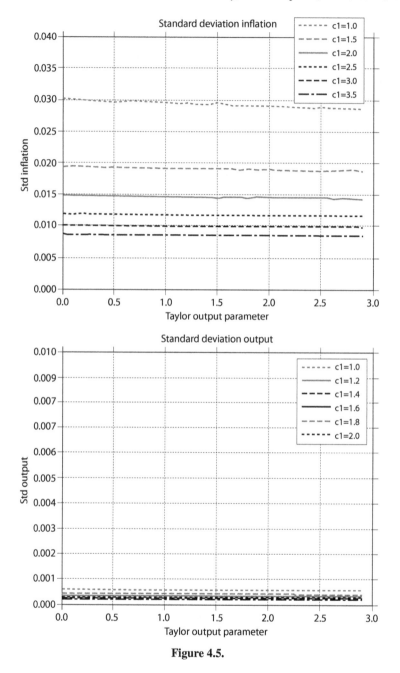

Figure 4.5.

increase in the interest rate on output declines. Note though that we need substantial increases in flexibility to produce this effect. An increase of b_2 from 0.05 to 0.5 does not seem to affect the impact of an interest rate shock on output.

The right-hand panels show the impulse responses of inflation to the same interest rate increase. Not surprisingly, more price flexibility leads to a stronger impact of an interest rate shock on inflation. In the limit as flexibility goes to infinity ($b_2 = \infty$) the interest rate shock only affects inflation, leaving output unchanged.

Finally, we also checked the trade-off between output and inflation variability in our behavioral model with perfect price flexibility. These are shown in figure 4.5. The upper panel shows the output variability (standard deviation) as a function of the Taylor output coefficient (c_2). It can be seen that we obtain horizontal lines. Thus output variability is unaffected by the degree of output stabilization performed by the central bank. In addition, the lines we obtain for different values of c_1 (the inflation parameter in the Taylor equation) coincide. This means that the central banks' responses to inflation do not affect the volatility of output. Put differently, output volatility is a real phenomenon and is unaffected by monetary policy actions.

The results are different for inflation variability (see second panel in figure 4.5). We observe first that as c_1 increases (the central bank reacts more forcefully to inflation), the degree of inflation volatility declines. Second, the degree of output stabilization (measured by c_2) does not have an impact on inflation volatility. The combination of the two panels in figure 4.5 leads to trade-offs (not shown) that are vertical with perfect price flexibility, implying that the central bank can only affect inflation variability and has no power to influence output variability. In such an environment, our behavioral model concludes in exactly the same way as the new classical model does, that strict inflation targeting is the best policy.

We conclude that our behavioral model leads to the same results as the standard new classical model when prices are perfectly flexible. As in the standard model, monetary policy has no real effects when prices adjust instantaneously (and when there are no other sources of inertia, e.g., habit formation of consumers). It only affects nominal variables (the rate of inflation). There is then also no scope for output stabilization and the best policy consists in keeping inflation low at all times. As is stressed in the new Keynesian models, it is the occurrence of price rigidity that provides a rationale for active monetary policy aimed at stabilizing output. In our model this rationale for stabilizing monetary policies is reinforced by animal spirits that can only emerge in an environment of price rigidities.

5

Animal Spirits and the Nature of Macroeconomic Shocks

5.1 Introduction

How important is the nature of the shocks hitting the economy? Macroeconomists have long recognized that demand and supply shocks have very different macroeconomic effects. In general, supply shocks are seen to be more uncomfortable. The main reason is that a supply shock moves inflation and output in opposite directions. A negative supply shock reduces output and increases inflation; a positive supply shock raises output and reduces inflation. This feature leads to an uncomfortable choice for the monetary authorities. They face a trade-off between stabilizing output and inflation. If, following a negative supply shock, they choose to fight inflation by raising the interest rate, they will have to sacrifice some output (at least in the short run).

No such trade-off exists when a demand shock hits the economy. In that case inflation and output move in the same direction. This makes life easier for the monetary authorities. Thus, if as a result of a positive demand shock inflation and output increase, they can reduce both by the same increase in the interest rate. This has led to the view that provided shocks are primarily demand shocks, a strict inflation targeting strategy will do a good job both at stabilizing inflation *and* output.

In this chapter we analyze the importance of the nature of the shocks in our behavioral macroeconomic model. We then discuss the policy implications. One question we will ask is whether strict inflation targeting is a good strategy when only demand shocks occur.

The way we proceed is to analyze the model first when only supply shocks exist, and then to do the same when only demand shocks. We then proceed by studying how strict inflation targeting is applied.

5.2 The Model with Only Supply or Demand Shocks

In this section we present the results of assuming that either only supply shocks occur, or only demand shocks. This will allow us to compare the characteristics of the model under those two extreme assumptions.

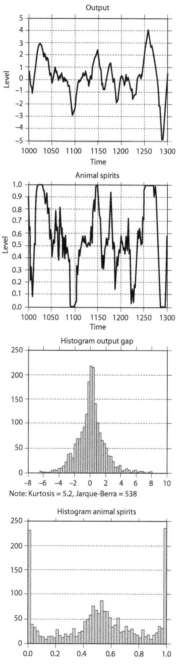

Figure 5.1. Only supply shocks.

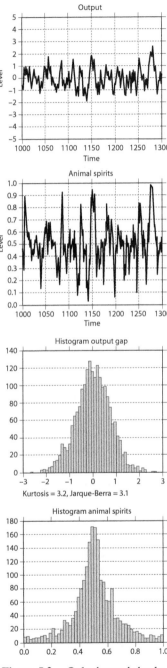

Figure 5.2. Only demand shocks.

In order to implement these assumptions we set the error term in the aggregate demand equation (1.1) equal to zero in the supply-shocks-only scenario. In the alternative scenario we set the error term in the supply equation (1.2) equal to zero. We present the results of simulating the model under these two scenarios in figures 5.1 and 5.2. The contrast is striking. When only supply shocks occur (figure 5.1), we obtain the results that we also found in chapter 1: there are strong cyclical movements in output gap; these cyclical movements are highly correlated with the animal spirits (correlation coefficient = 0.89); the output gap is not normally distributed and this feature is related to the fact that the markets are regularly gripped by extreme optimism or extreme pessimism.

These results are very different from those found in the scenario where only demand shocks occur (figure 5.2). In this case the cyclical movements of the output gap are much weaker and show much less amplitude. Animal spirits are a weak force. There are never moments where everybody is either an optimist or a pessimist. The result of all this is that the output gap is normally distributed, and the market is never gripped by extreme optimism and pessimism. Thus when only demand shocks occur we obtain results that come very close to the mainstream rational expectations new Keynesian model.

How can these striking differences be explained? The answer has to do with what was noted earlier. In the demand-shocks-only scenario, the central bank has an easy job in stabilizing both inflation and output. There is never a choice to be made. This has the effect that by stabilizing output and inflation, the animal spirits are also "tamed," so that extreme optimism or pessimism have no chance to emerge. (Note that the Taylor rule equation applies and we impose the same coefficients as in chapter 1.)

In the supply-shocks-only scenario, the central bank faces the difficult trade-off between stabilizing inflation and output. As a result, stabilization is very imperfect, giving scope for animal spirits to do their work in destabilizing output.

It is also useful to look at how inflation behaves in the two scenarios. We show this in figure 5.3. The left-hand panel shows the rate of inflation in the supply-shocks-only scenario; the right-hand panel in the demand-shocks-only scenario. Again the contrast is striking. In the demand-shocks-only scenario the central bank is extremely successful in stabilizing inflation. In the supply-shocks-only scenario, inflation is very volatile, mainly as a result of the extreme volatility of the animal spirits. Note that in the two scenarios we assume exactly the same coefficients in the Taylor rule.

It is important to understand that the success at stabilizing inflation in the demand-shocks-only scenario arises from the fact that the central bank attempts to stabilize both inflation and the output gap. In order to illustrate this we simulated the demand-shocks-only scenario assuming strict inflation targeting. The latter means that the central bank does not aim at stabilizing output (the output coefficient in the Taylor

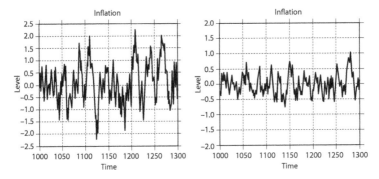

Figure 5.3. Inflation under two scenarios: supply-shocks-only (left-hand panel); demand-shocks-only (right-hand panel).

rule is zero). Is this strict inflation targeting sufficient to stabilize output if the shocks only come from the demand side? One may think that the answer is positive since inflation and output are positively correlated when only demand shocks occur. Stabilizing inflation then also stabilizes output. Is this also the case in our behavioral model? The answer is given in figure 5.4. We now observe that the output gap becomes much more volatile and that animal spirits become the main driving force behind this volatility. Animal spirits now switch between extreme optimism and pessimism. This can also be seen in the lower two panels of figure 5.4. The output gap now ceases to be normally distributed and this is due to the extreme values animal spirits regularly take. Thus we are back in the world of nonnormality, despite the fact that shocks only occur in the demand equation. The reason we obtain this result is that the central bank applies strict inflation targeting thereby allowing animal spirits to be set loose and to destabilize output and inflation. Thus, the existence of only demand shocks is no excuse for not explicitly stabilizing output (in addition to stabilizing inflation).

Put differently, the reason why we found earlier that in a world where only demand shocks occur animal spirits are a weak force has to do with the fact that we assumed that the central bank explicitly stabilizes output. When the central bank eliminates its ambition to stabilize output (strict inflation targeting), animal spirits become a strong force again.

The importance of applying output stabilization even when there exist only demand shocks is also made vivid by studying the trade-offs obtained in the two scenarios. We analyze these trade-offs in the next two sections.

5.3 Trade-offs in the Supply-Shocks-Only Scenario

In this section we present the trade-offs between inflation and output variability in the supply-shocks-only scenario. These trade-offs are constructed in the same way as in chapter 3. We show the results in figure 5.5. We obtain qualitatively

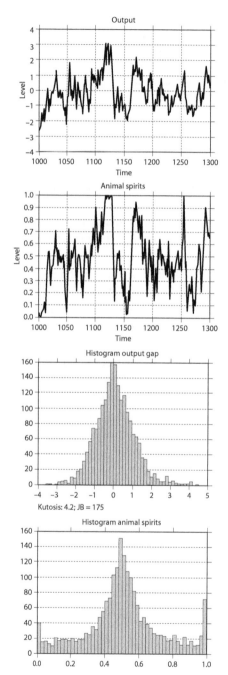

Figure 5.4. Demand-shocks-only scenario and strict inflation targeting.

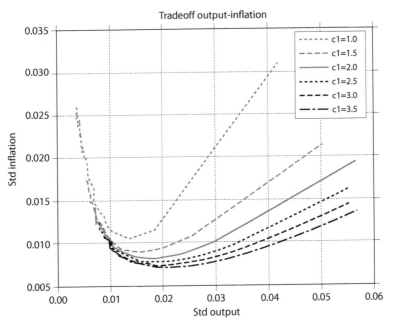

Figure 5.5. Trade-offs: supply-shocks-only scenario.

similar results as in the standard scenarios with shocks in both the demand and supply equations, i.e., there is a nonlinearity in the trade-off. We have explained this feature in chapter 3. To repeat, it implies that strict inflation targeting is never optimal. Some output stabilization reduces both inflation and output volatility. Too much output stabilization is not desirable, however. When applying too much output stabilization the trade-off becomes negatively sloped. This means that further output stabilization comes at a price, in the form of less inflation stability.

We can also derive the relationship between the credibility of inflation targeting and the degree of output stabilization as we have done in chapter 3. We show this in figure 5.6. We find that starting from zero, an increase in the Taylor output coefficient increases the credibility of inflation targeting. Up to a point. When too much output stabilization is applied, credibility starts declining.

5.4 Trade-offs in the Demand-Shocks-Only Scenario

We obtain very different trade-offs when shocks occur only in the demand curve. We show these trade-offs in figure 5.7. The striking feature of these trade-offs is that they are positively sloped throughout. This means that, when only demand shocks occur, applying output stabilization reduces both inflation and output volatility. Conversely, reducing the degree of output stabilization increases both inflation and output volatility. In a way this is not surprising. When only demand shocks occur, output and inflation are positively correlated. No trade-off arises for the central

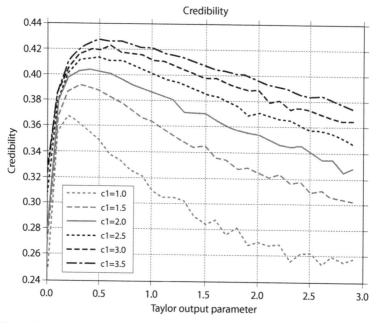

Figure 5.6. Credibility of inflation targeting in the supply-shocks-only scenario.

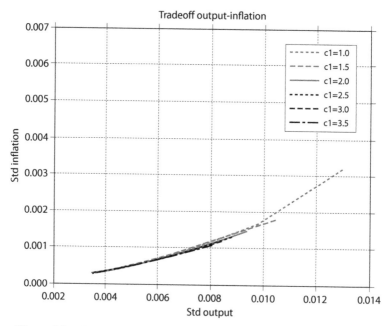

Figure 5.7. Trade-offs: demand-shocks-only scenario in behavioral model.

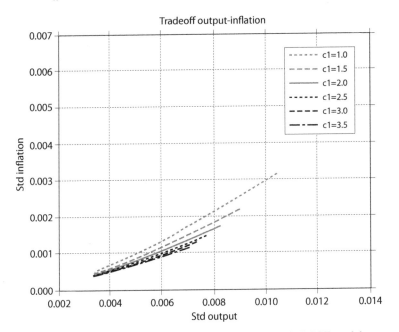

Figure 5.8. Trade-offs: demand-shocks-only scenario in DSGE model.

bank. This result also holds in the rational expectations (DSGE) model. We show this in figure 5.8. Thus, in both models it pays to stabilize output. In the behavioral model, however, there is an additional dimension to this. We have noted earlier that what makes stabilization of demand shocks important in the behavioral model is the fact that it eliminates the fat tails in the distribution of the output gap. Put differently, it makes it possible to avoid the large booms and busts. This is not visible from the trade-offs in figure 5.7 because these only take into account the second moment of the distribution of inflation and output, not the higher moments.

In order to shed more light on the importance of output stabilization as a tool to reduce the fat tails in the distribution of the output gap we computed the Jarque–Bera statistic (JBstat) for different values of the output parameter in the Taylor equation. This statistic tests for normality of the distribution. The critical value is around 3. When JBstat exceeds 3 one can reject the hypothesis that the distribution of the output gap is normal. We plot the results in figure 5.9. We find that for values of the Taylor output parameter less than 0.5, the distribution of the output gap is nonnormal. Thus when the central bank does not apply enough stabilization ($c_2 < 0.5$), the distribution of the output gap exhibits fat tails, i.e., there will regularly be large booms and busts in output. This can be avoided by applying a sufficient amount of output stabilization ($c_2 > 0.5$). In that case the central bank does not give a chance to animal spirits to "show their ugly heads," and to trigger large booms and busts. Note that the amount of stabilization that has to be applied

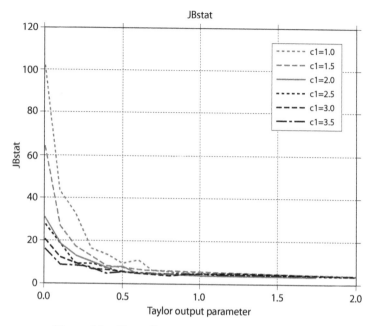

Figure 5.9. Normality test for different values of Taylor
output parameter when only demand shocks occur.

is not that large, and that it corresponds to what we observe central banks do. Econometric evidence suggests that c_2 is close to 0.5 for major central banks (see Taylor 1993).

Finally, we also show the relation between the credibility of inflation targeting and the degree of output stabilization in figure 5.10. In contrast with the results of the previous section, this is now a positively sloped relationship (although leveling off when the output parameter increases). Thus, more intense output stabilization always improves the credibility of inflation targeting when there are only demand shocks.

5.5   Conclusion

In this chapter we have analyzed the importance of shocks in generating the dynamics of animal spirits. We have seen that when there are only supply shocks animal spirits are an endemic feature of macroeconomic dynamics. This has to do with the fact that supply shocks create an unpleasant trade-off for monetary authorities which reduces their capacity to "tame the animal spirits." Such an unpleasant trade-off does not exist when there are only demand shocks. This does not mean that in a world where only demand shocks exist it is sufficient for central bankers to only target the rate of inflation (strict inflation targeting). We showed that if central bankers apply strict inflation targeting, animal spirits reappear even when

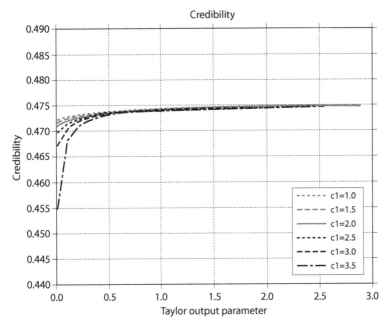

Figure 5.10. Credibility of inflation targeting in the demand-shocks-only scenario.

only demand shocks occur. This reinforces the conclusion arrived at in chapter 3 that strict inflation targeting is never optimal.

The conclusion that strict inflation targeting is never optimal even when only demand shocks occurs contrasts with the conclusion obtained in new Keynesian rational expectations models. In the latter model one finds that in the absence of a trade-off between output and inflation variability strict inflation is optimal, i.e., all a central bank has to do is to stabilize the price level. This will automatically also stabilize output. In our behavioral model this is no longer the case.

6

Stock Prices and Monetary Policy

6.1 Introduction

Since the eruption of the financial crisis in 2007 it has become clear that asset markets are important for understanding macroeconomic fluctuations. Stock markets, bond markets, and real estate markets are regularly gripped by speculative fever leading to bubbles and crashes.[1] These movements affect fluctuations of output and inflation. In this chapter we introduce asset markets in our macroeconomic model. We will analyze two issues. The first one is the issue of how asset markets interact with movements in output and inflation. Do these asset markets intensify cyclical movements in output and inflation? And how does the goods market in turn affect the asset markets?

The second issue we will study is whether and how central banks should react to asset price developments. Should they try to limit the movements in asset prices, or are these better left free and determined by market forces?

6.2 Introducing Asset Prices in the Behavioral Model

In this section we describe how asset prices enter the model. These asset prices will be assumed to be stock prices. We allow the stock prices to affect aggregate demand and supply.

Let us first concentrate on the *aggregate demand* effect of changes in stock prices. There are two mechanisms through which a change in stock prices affects aggregate demand (for a concise treatment see Burda and Wyplosz (2009)). The first mechanism arises as a result of a wealth effect, i.e., when stock prices increase, the wealth of consumers increases and this leads them to spend more on consumption goods. The second effect has been made popular by Bernanke and Gertler (1995), who introduced the concept of credit amplification. The starting point is that when firms want to borrow they face the fact that the lenders, say the banks, are not fully informed about the risks of the investment projects of the firm. Thus, a firm that wants to borrow from the bank will have to pay a risk premium. This is called the

---

[1] For a classic analysis of the history of bubbles and crashes, see Kindleberger (2000). See also Minsky (1986) and Goodhart and Hoffmann (2004).

external finance premium of the firm. The greater the perceived risk the higher will be this external finance premium.

Movements in stock prices can now be shown to affect the external risk premium. An increase in the stock price of the firm increases its net equity. As a result, banks perceive the risk of lending to the firm to have declined. The external finance premium declines. This makes banks more willing to lend. Credit becomes more easily available for the firm, stimulating investment demand.

Changes in stock prices also affect *aggregate supply*. The mechanism goes through the same external risk premium effect of a change in the stock prices. Thus when the stock prices increase the external risk premium declines. The latter then in turn reduces the firm's credit costs. Since firms have to hold working capital to be able to pay workers and suppliers, this decline in credit costs lowers the marginal costs of the firm. Aggregate supply will be stimulated.

These demand and supply side effects can also be labeled balance sheet effects of stock price changes. An increase in stock prices improves the balance sheet of the firm allowing it to increase its spending for investment at a lower cost and to run its operations at a lower (credit) cost. As it is a balance sheet effect we will introduce a lag in its operation, i.e., an increase in the stock price in period t improves the published balance sheet at the end of period t, allowing the firm to profit from the improved balance sheet in the next period.

Clearly, a decline in the stock price has the reverse effect on the balance sheets of firms, leading to a negative effect on investment spending and on the credit costs.

We use the popular discounted dividend model (Gordon model[2]) to compute stock prices, i.e.,

$$S_t = \frac{E_t(D_{t+1})}{R_t}, \tag{6.1}$$

where $E_t(D_{t+1})$ is the expected future dividend, which is assumed to be constant from $t+1$ onwards; R_t is the discount rate used to compute the present value of future dividends. It consists of the interest rate r_t and the equity premium (which we will assume to be constant). Thus we assume that each period agents make a forecast of the future dividends that they assume will then be constant for the indefinite future. They reevaluate this forecast every period.

Dividends are a fraction, α, of nominal GDP. Thus the forecasts of future dividends are tightly linked to the forecasts of output gap and inflation that we discussed in chapter 1.

We now specify the aggregate demand curve as follows:

$$y_t = a_1 \tilde{E}_t y_{t+1} + (1 - a_1) y_{t-1} + a_2(r_t - \tilde{E}_t \pi_{t+1}) + a_3 \Delta s_{t-1} + \varepsilon_t, \tag{6.2}$$

where Δs_{t-1} is the change in the log of S_{t-1} and $a_3 \geqslant 0$.

---

[2] For a discussion see, for example, Brealy and Myers (1984).

Compared with the aggregate demand curve introduced in chapter 1 we now have added one variable, the change in the stock prices. The latter is assumed to have a positive effect on aggregate demand for the reasons spelled out earlier, i.e., a boom in stock prices tends to stimulate aggregate demand.

The aggregate supply (new Keynesian Phillips curve) is specified as follows:

$$\pi_t = b_1 \tilde{E}_t \pi_{t+1} + (1 - b_1)\pi_{t-1} + b_2 y_t + b_3 \Delta s_{t-1} + \eta_t, \tag{6.3}$$

where $b_3 \leqslant 0$, i.e., an increase in the stock prices lowers marginal costs and thus has a negative effect on inflation.

Finally, we will allow the central bank to react to changes in the stock prices. Thus the Taylor rule becomes

$$r_t = c_1(\pi_t - \pi_t^*) + c_2 y_t + c_3 r_{t-1} + c_4 \Delta s_{t-1} + u_t. \tag{6.4}$$

Note that we specify the way the central bank reacts to stock prices in a different way to the way it reacts to inflation and output. In the latter case, the central bank has a target for inflation and output and wishes to reduce deviations from that target.[3] In the case of stock prices, the central bank has no target for stock prices. Instead, it follows a "leaning against the wind" strategy. This is the way proponents of central banks' involvement in the stock market usually formulate the central bank's strategy. The reason is that there is no generally accepted body of economic theory allowing us to determine what the best level is for share prices.

The forecasts of output gap and inflation are governed by the same selection mechanism as the one described in chapter 1. In this extended version of the behavioral model agents also have to forecast future dividends. These forecasts then determine the stock price through equation (6.1). We assume dividends to be a constant fraction of nominal output (GDP). Since nominal output has a price and quantity component the forecasts of inflation and output add up to a forecast of nominal output. Thus the change in the stock price Δs_t is determined by the forecasts of inflation and output. We will use the same expectations formation process as the one spelled out in the chapter 1. We will, however, continue to focus on the output gap, i.e., GDP minus capacity GDP. This also means that we take out the trend from GDP. As a result, the stock prices will not show a trend either.

A methodological note is in place here. We have not tried to derive the aggregate demand and supply equations from micro-founded principles. We explained earlier (see chapter 1) why this cannot easily be done. To repeat: developments in psychology and brain sciences have made it clear that the assumption of individual agents who maximize an intertemporal utility function using all available information should be rejected (Kahneman 2011). Thus the micro-foundation used in

---

[3] This may not be obvious for the output gap. The output gap is the difference between observed output and capacity (natural) output. Thus implicit in the Taylor rule is the idea that the central bank wants to minimize the deviation of observed output from capacity output (the target).

mainstream macroeconomic models cannot be the right one. Our brains function in a different way. Unfortunately, we do not know sufficiently about how our brains function to provide a satisfactory micro-foundation.

6.3 Simulating the Model

We use the same parameters as in chapter 1. We first show the results of a simulation exercise in which, as before, the three shocks (demand shocks, supply shocks, and interest rate shocks) are i.i.d. with standard deviations of 0.5%. In the first set of simulations we assume that the central bank does not attempt to influence the stock prices, i.e., $c_4 = 0$. We will analyze the implications of allowing the central bank to react to changes in the stock price in section 6.4.

We first present a simulation in the time domain. Figure 6.1 shows the time pattern of output gap, stock prices, and animal spirits produced by the model. As in chapter 1, we observe a strong cyclical movement in the output gap. The source of these cyclical movements is seen to be the index of animal spirits in the market (see second panel of figure 6.1). As in chapter 1 endogenous waves of optimism and pessimism are highly correlated with movements in the output gap. During some periods pessimists dominate and this translates into below average output growth. These pessimistic periods are followed by optimistic ones when optimistic forecasts tend to dominate and the growth rate of output is above average.

The third panel of figure 6.1 shows the evolution of the stock prices in the time domain. The model creates periods of bullish and bearish behavior of the stock prices that are associated with the same waves of optimism and pessimism (second panel). The model is also capable of creating bubbles and crashes in the stock market.[4]

These endogenously generated cycles in output and stock prices are made possible by a self-fulfilling mechanism that was described in chapter 1. A series of random shocks creates the possibility that one of the two forecasting rules, say the optimistic one, delivers a higher payoff, i.e., a lower mean squared forecast error (MSFE). This attracts agents who were using the pessimistic rule. The "contagion effect" leads to an increasing use of the optimistic belief to forecast the output gap, which in turn stimulates aggregate demand and leads to a bullish stock market. Optimism is therefore self-fulfilling. A boom is created. In this case there is also an interaction between the stock market and the goods market. The booms in these two markets tend to reinforce each other. At some point, negative stochastic shocks make a dent in the MSFE of the optimistic forecasts. The pessimistic belief becomes

---

[4] Note that with "bubbles" we do not refer to the rational bubbles obtained in rational expectations models. In fact, in mainstream DSGE models these rational bubbles are usually excluded by imposing transversality conditions. Here we refer to developments in asset prices that are dissociated from the underlying fundamentals. They arise when extrapolative forecasting dominates in the markets.

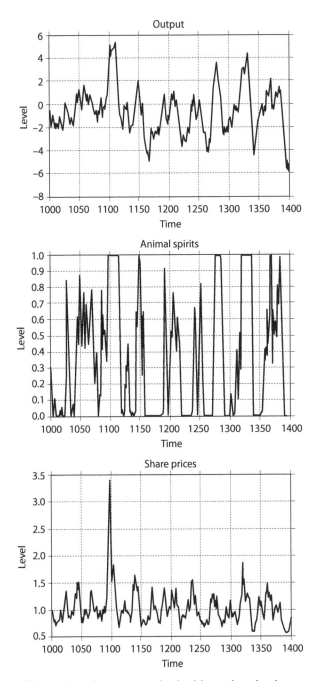

Figure 6.1. Output gap, animal spirits, and stock prices.

attractive and therefore fashionable again. The stock market and the economy turn around. The same kind of interaction then occurs but working in the other direction.

It is useful to compare the dynamics of the model that includes stock prices with the model of chapter 1 that does not include stock prices. We do this in figure 6.2. The contrast between the two models is quite striking. In the asset market model we obtain longer waves of optimism and pessimism leading to larger movements in the output gap than in the model without asset prices. This can be seen from the time series results of the output gap and animal spirits. It is confirmed by the frequency distribution of the output gap exhibiting fatter tails in the asset market model and from the frequency distribution of the animal spirits that has more concentration of observations in the extremes of optimism and pessimism in the asset market model (note that the scales of the vertical axes differ).

Thus animal spirits affect both the stock prices and the output gap. This also leads to a reinforcing interaction where booms in the stock market reinforce the sense of optimism (euphoria) thereby strengthening the boom in the output gap which feeds back again into the stock market.

6.4   Should the Central Bank Care about Stock Prices?

The question of whether central banks should react to stock price developments has been hotly debated. It is fair to state that there are two schools of thought on this issue. The first one, which is well represented by Bernanke and Gertler (2001), Bernanke (2003), Schwartz (2002), Bean (2003), and Greenspan (2007), argues that central banks should not use the interest rate to influence stock prices. The main arguments advanced by this school of thought are, first, that it is difficult to identify bubbles *ex ante* (and it only makes sense to intervene if stock prices are on a bubble path, i.e., if they clearly deviate from underlying fundamentals).[5] The second argument is that even if a bubble can be identified *ex ante*, using the interest rate is ineffective to burst a bubble. All the central bank can do is to limit the damage once the bubble bursts. This school of thought also stresses that by keeping the rate of inflation low, the central bank contributes to creating an environment of sustainable growth in which bubbles are less likely to emerge.[6]

The second school of thought takes the opposite view (see Smets 1997; Cecchetti et al. 2000; Borio and White 2004; Bordo and Jeanne 2002; Roubini 2006). Stock prices are often subject to bubbles and crashes. These can have strong pro-cyclical

---

[5] An extreme version of this school of thought denies the existence of bubbles altogether. In this view, financial markets are efficient and thus stock prices always reflect the best available information. Since central banks do not posses better information than markets, it makes no sense for them to try to influence stock prices.

[6] It is also worth mentioning that an argument against targeting asset prices is that changes in the latter are reflected in the rate of inflation. This, however, does not need to be the case. A positive productivity shock, for example, typically shifts aggregate demand and supply positively, leaving the price level pretty much unchanged. Such a productivity shock, however, can easily trigger a bubble in asset prices.

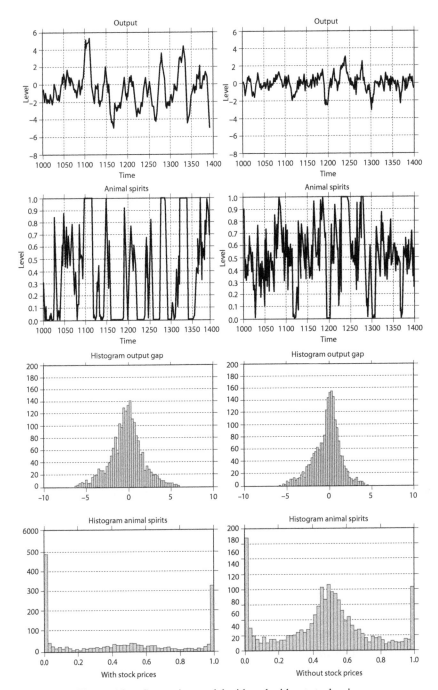

Figure 6.2. Comparing model with and without stock prices.

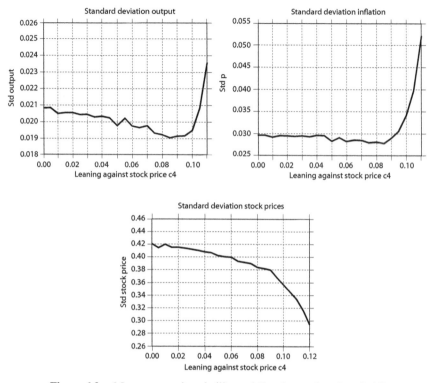

Figure 6.3.   Macroeconomic volatility and "leaning against the wind."

effects and can also affect the stability of financial markets. Since central banks are responsible for financial stability they should monitor asset prices and try to prevent the emergence of bubbles (that invariably lead to crashes). In this view the use of the interest rate is seen as effective in preventing bubbles from emerging.[7] Few economists from this school will argue that the central bank should target a particular value of the stock price (in the same way as it targets an inflation rate). Instead, many will argue that a strategy of "leaning against the wind" may be useful for reducing too strong movements in stock prices.

In this section we analyze the issue of the effectiveness of a leaning-against-the-wind strategy used by the central bank to limit the fluctuations in the stock prices. We will ask the question of whether this strategy improves the central bank's capacity for stabilizing output and inflation. Thus, we take the view that attempts to reduce stock price fluctuations should be gauged by the success they have in reducing inflation and output volatility.

---

[7] Note that both schools of thought accept that the central bank has other instruments to maintain financial stability, e.g., supervision and regulation.

The way we attempt to answer this question is as follows. We simulated the model under different assumptions about the intensity of the leaning-against-the-wind strategy in the stock market as measured by the coefficient c_4 in the Taylor rule equation. We selected values of c_4 ranging from 0 to 0.12. For each of these parameter values we simulated the model over 1000 periods and computed the standard deviations of output, inflation, and stock prices. We repeated this exercise 100 times and computed the mean standard deviations obtained for each value of c_4. We show the results in figure 6.3. We observe the following. As c_4 increases the standard deviations of output, inflation, and stock prices decline. At some point, i.e., when c_4 comes close to 0.1, the standard deviations of output and inflation increase dramatically, while the standard deviation of the stock prices declines significantly. Thus, as long as the leaning-against-the-wind strategy is moderate, this strategy pays off and reduces the volatility of inflation, output, and stock prices. When this strategy becomes too active (too large a value of c_4), it creates additional volatility in inflation and output. We conclude that mild forms of reacting to stock price developments can be effective in reducing macroeconomic volatility.

This conclusion is of the same nature as our conclusion about output stabilization in chapter 3. There we found that some output stabilization is good because it reduces output and inflation volatility. Too much ambition in output stabilization, however, leads to losses in credibility and undermines the stabilization effort. We obtain a similar result about the stabilizing properties of asset price stabilization efforts.

6.5 Inflation Targeting and Macroeconomic Stability

Our previous analysis was conducted in an environment of inflation targeting in which, however, agents maintained their skepticism about the credibility of the inflation-targeting regime. As a result, as we have seen, the inflation rate occasionally departs from its target in a substantial way. Thus we modeled a regime of imperfect credibility of the inflation target.

In this section we analyze two extreme cases concerning the credibility of the inflation target. One is to assume that there is 100% credibility; the other assumption is that there is no credibility at all. We take these two extremes, not because these are particularly realistic, but rather to focus on how different degrees of credibility affect macroeconomic stability and the capacity of the monetary authorities to enhance stability by leaning-against-the-wind strategies in the stock markets.

We model these two extremes as follows. In the perfect credibility regime we assume that all agents perceive the central bank's announced inflation target π^* to be fully credible. They use this value as their forecast of future inflation, i.e., $\tilde{E}_t \pi_{t+1} = \pi^*$. Since all agents believe this, they do not switch to the alternative forecasting rule of extrapolating the past inflation rate (see also chapter 1 on this).

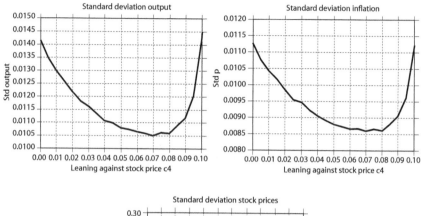

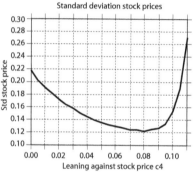

Figure 6.4. Macroeconomic volatility when inflation target is 100% credible.

The other extreme case, i.e., zero credibility of the inflation target, is modeled symmetrically. Now no agent attaches any credibility to the announced inflation target, and therefore each of them is an "extrapolator." As before, this is defined by $\tilde{E}_t^{\text{ext}} \pi_{t+1} = \pi_{t-1}$. In this case there is also no switching to the alternative forecasting rule.

We show the results of these two exercises in figures 6.4 and 6.5. Let us concentrate on figure 6.4 first, showing the degree of macroeconomic volatility in a regime of 100% credibility of the inflation target. Note first that in the regime of full credibility of the inflation target the volatility of the output, inflation, and stock prices is significantly lower than in the regime of the imperfectly credible inflation target. The difference is quite high. Comparing figure 6.4 with figure 6.3 shows that in a fully credible inflation targeting regime the standard deviations of output, inflation, and stock prices are about half as large as in the case of imperfect credibility. Thus, credibility is extremely valuable. It allows the reduction of the volatility of all three macroeconomic variables, at no apparent cost. This result is very much in line with the results obtained in chapter 1.

A second conclusion from a comparison of figures 6.4 and 6.3 is that mild forms of leaning against the wind in the stock market have a much stronger effect in

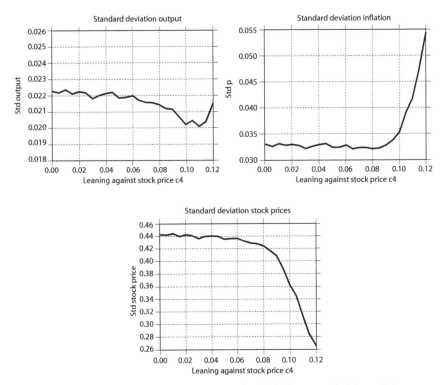

Figure 6.5. Macroeconomic volatility when inflation target is 0% credible.

reducing volatility of output, inflation, and stock prices when credibility is perfect. Thus, credibility of the inflation target makes leaning against the wind in the stock markets more effective in reducing macroeconomic volatility. (Note again that this only holds for relatively low levels of c_4.)

The importance of credibility as a means to achieving macroeconomic stability and as a way of making leaning against the wind in the stock market an effective stabilization tool is reinforced by the results of figure 6.5. These show that when there is total absence of credibility in the inflation target, the volatility of output, inflation, and stock prices is higher for all values of c_4. In addition, leaning against the wind in the stock market now has almost no stabilizing properties for output and inflation (compare figure 6.5 with figure 6.3).

6.6 The Trade-off between Output and Inflation Variability

Another way to evaluate leaning-against-the-wind strategies in the stock markets is to analyze how they affect the trade-off between output and inflation variability. We will proceed as follows. We return to the regime of the imperfectly credible inflation target. We assume several values of c_4 from 0 to 0.05 (the leaning-against-the-wind parameter in the stock market). We then compute the trade-offs between output and

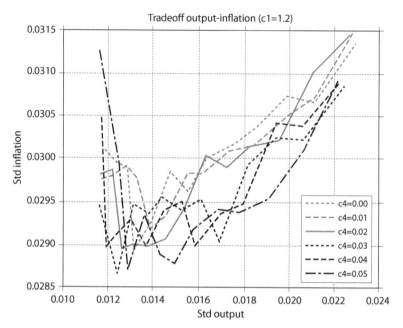

Figure 6.6. Trade-off between output and inflation variability: imperfect credibility.

inflation variability in the same way as we did in chapter 3.[8] We plot the results in figures 6.6.

A first important finding concerns the shape of these trade-offs. As in chapter 3, we find that these trade-offs are nonlinear, i.e., there is a positively and a negatively sloped segment. It is worth repeating the interpretation here. When the central bank does not care about output stabilization ($c_2 = 0$) we are located in the upper right points of the trade-offs. An increase in the willingness to stabilize output (c_2 increases) leads to a downward movement along the trade-off. This means that when the central bank increases its output stabilization effort it reduces both the variability of output and inflation. At some point, however, applying more stabilization (c_2 increases further) brings us in the upward sloping part. From then on more stabilization leads to the traditional trade-off: more output stability is bought by more inflation variability. This is the standard result obtained in rational expectations models (see chapter 3). In these models any attempt to stabilize output leads to more inflation variability. In our behavioral model this is not necessarily the case. Mild forms of output stabilization (low c_2) have the effect of reducing both output and inflation variability. When, however, the ambition to stabilize output

---

[8] That is, we allow the output stabilization parameter (c_2) in the Taylor rule to increase from 0 to 1 and compute the standard deviations of output and inflation for each value of c_2. Note that the output stabilization coefficient has much larger values than the stock price coefficient (c_4). This has to do with the fact that the variations in stock prices per unit of time are a multiple of the variations in the output gap.

is too strong, we return to the traditional negatively sloped trade-off and the gain in output stabilization leads to more inflation variability. Thus, in our model some output stabilization is always better than no stabilization at all. This result comes from the structure of our model. When the central bank applies modest output stabilization it also reduces the correlation of biased beliefs and the ensuing waves of optimism and pessimism. The latter affect not only output variability but also inflation variability. Thus by reducing these "animal spirits" the central bank achieves both lower output and inflation variability. It can do this because it profits from a credibility bonus. Too much activism, however, destroys this credibility bonus, leading to the normal negatively sloped trade-offs.

A second finding from figure 6.6 relates to the effect of leaning against the wind in the stock market. We find that a more intense leaning against the wind in the stock market improves the trade-offs, i.e., shifts them downwards. Thus leaning against the wind reduces both output and inflation variability. Note, however, that this result only holds in the positively sloped segment of the trade-offs. In the negatively sloped part, there is no clear effect of leaning-against-the-wind strategies. This suggests that leaning-against-the-wind strategies are effective in reducing both output and inflation variability for the same reason as output stabilization does. These strategies tend to reduce the scope for waves of optimism and pessimism and thus stabilize the macroeconomy as a whole. A too aggressive use of these strategies, however, will tend to create an inflationary bias, which then reestablishes the negative trade-off between output and inflation variability.

As in the previous section we analyzed the importance of the credibility of inflation. We do this by assuming the same two extreme regimes, perfect credibility and zero credibility. The perfect credibility case is shown in figure 6.7. It confirms some of the results obtained earlier. For example, the trade-offs under perfect credibility are located much lower than those obtained under imperfect credibility (compare figure 6.7 with figure 6.6). Thus, credibility dramatically improves the trade-offs, leading to less variability of both output and inflation. We also find that leaning-against-the-wind strategies improve these trade-offs significantly, thus lowering both output and inflation variability.

The case of zero credibility of inflation target is shown in figure 6.8. The contrast with the previous figures is striking. The trade-offs are located higher than in the previous two cases, and the positive segments of the trade-offs have practically disappeared. This has to do with the fact that in the absence of any credibility in the inflation target, agents quickly punish the central bank by extrapolating the higher inflation that results from active stabilization policies. We also conclude from figure 6.8 that leaning-against-the-wind strategies have no visible impact on the trade-offs. Thus policies aiming at reducing the volatility of asset prices by manipulating the interest rates do not improve macroeconomic stability when inflation targeting has no credibility.

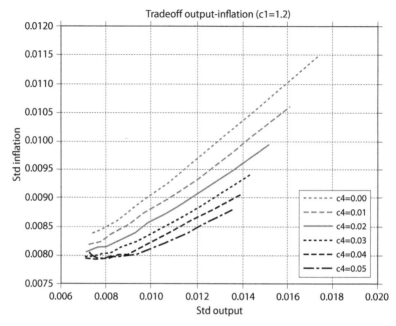

Figure 6.7.   Trade-off between output and inflation variability: perfect credibility.

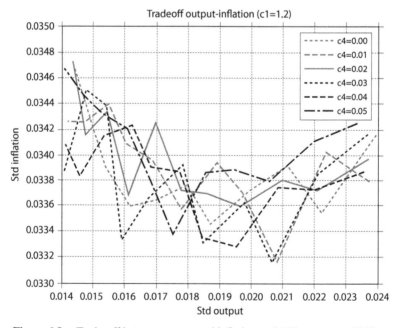

Figure 6.8.   Trade-off between output and inflation variability: zero credibility.

6.7 Conclusion

Should central banks use their interest rate instrument to influence the asset prices and to prevent bubbles from emerging? Economists have hotly debated this question. It has become topical again since the credit crisis erupted in August 2007. We analyzed this question using our behavioral macroeconomic model. This model produces booms and busts that arise from the fact that biased beliefs about the future become correlated (animal spirits). As we showed in this chapter, the interaction of booms and busts in the stock market and in the goods markets tends to increase macroeconomic volatility in output and inflation. It is therefore quite legitimate to analyze the question of whether the central bank should take stock price movements into account when deciding about monetary policies.

Our main results are the following. Yes, central banks can influence stock prices, and by following leaning-against-the-wind strategies in the stock market they can improve the trade-off between output and inflation, i.e., they can reduce the volatility of both output and inflation. They achieve this result because they help to reduce the correlation in biased beliefs and the ensuing booms and busts. This result, however, only holds in an environment of credible inflation targeting. If the inflation target has a high degree of credibility, we find that these leaning-against-the-wind strategies significantly improve macroeconomic stability (output and inflation stability). However, these policies aiming at reducing the volatility of asset prices by manipulating the interest rates do not improve macroeconomic stability when inflation targeting has no credibility.

Thus there is a grain of truth in the two schools of thought about the desirability of targeting stock prices. As mentioned earlier, the first school of thought stresses the importance of price stability. Our results confirm this insight. At the same time, our results also confirm the insights of the second school of thought stressing that central banks can and should try to influence asset prices as part of their strategy of minimizing macroeconomic volatility.

One limitation of the present analysis is that this chapter considers the use of only one instrument, the interest rate, for influencing inflation, output, and asset prices. Modern central banks, however, have other instruments at their disposal that they could use to affect asset prices. These additional instruments include minimum reserve requirements and other tools to affect the banks' capacity to lend.[9] The use of additional instruments would facilitate achieving both price stability and stability in asset prices.

---

[9] See De Grauwe and Gros (2009), who propose a two-pillar strategy for central banks. One pillar would consist in using the interest rate to target inflation and output and another pillar that would use reserve requirements to target bank loans. The latter are often the driving forces behind the bubbles in asset prices (see Borio and White 2004).

7

Extensions of the Basic Model

The behavioral model developed in the previous chapters used very simple heuristics. Agents who are forecasting the output gap were either fundamentalists or extrapolators. The use of these simple rules allowed us to derive powerful results. The issue that arises, however, is whether or not these results are too dependent on the specific rules used. Put differently, if we had used other rules, would we still have obtained the same or similar results? This is the issue of the robustness of the results. The problem of the robustness of the results in a behavioral model is quite fundamental. It does not occur in the same way in the mainstream models with full rational behavior because there is only one way to be rational. Once we depart from full rationality, there are many ways one can model this departure (see Holland and Miller 1991) on this.

The way we will analyze this issue is by introducing other rules (heuristics) assuming the same type of selection mechanism between these rules as the one we have been using up to now. Thus we extend the menu of simple rules agents can use and analyze how these new menus affects the results.

7.1 Fundamentalists Are Biased

The behavioral model assumes that the fundamentalists know the equilibrium value of the output gap and use this knowledge to make forecasts. We will now drop this assumption and instead take the view that fundamentalists who do not observe the equilibrium output gap are uncertain about the true value of the output gap.

It is useful here to pause again and to think about the meaning of uncertainty. Using the distinction introduced by Frank Knight (see chapter 1), uncertainty has two meanings. The first one is uncertainty in the sense of risk. This is the uncertainty that can be quantified and that allows agents to make probabilistic statements based on a statistical analysis of past movements of the output gap. This is the meaning to uncertainty given in mainstream macroeconomic models. In such a model agents will do a statistical analysis of past movements of the output gap and base their forecasts on a continuous updating of the statistical information.

The second meaning of uncertainty is an uncertainty that cannot be quantified and that therefore does not allow agents to make probabilistic statements. This is the meaning of uncertainty that we will use here. Agents in our model take the view that the movements of the output gap are not normally distributed and that there is too much fat tail risk that they cannot quantify (see chapter 1 on this). They therefore use simple but biased heuristics to estimate the equilibrium output gap.

We will assume the simplest possible heuristic. This is that some agents are overly optimistic in estimating the equilibrium output gap, i.e., they exhibit an optimistic bias; other agents are too pessimistic and exhibit a pessimistic bias. We now obtain the following equations:

the optimistic fundamentalist rule (fo) is defined by

$$\tilde{E}_t^{\text{fo}} y_{t+1} = a, \qquad (7.1)$$

the pessimistic fundamentalist rule (fp) is defined by

$$\tilde{E}_t^{\text{fp}} y_{t+1} = -a, \qquad (7.2)$$

where a is a positive constant.

Thus the optimists systematically overestimate the equilibrium output gap while the pessimists systematically underestimate it. We assume that the bias is symmetrical.

Since we also have an extrapolative rule, which was defined as

$$\tilde{E}_t^{\text{e}} y_{t+1} = y_{t-1}, \qquad (7.3)$$

we obtain a model with three rules.

As before, a selection mechanism is assumed, whereby agents can switch between the three rules. This implies first that agents compute the performance (utility) of using these rules as in chapter 1:

performance of optimistic fundamentalist rule:

$$U_{\text{fo},t} = -\sum_{k=0}^{\infty} \omega_k [y_{t-k-1} - \tilde{E}_{\text{fo},t-k-2} y_{t-k-1}]^2,$$

performance of pessimistic fundamentalist rule:

$$U_{\text{fp},t} = -\sum_{k=0}^{\infty} \omega_k [y_{t-k-1} - \tilde{E}_{\text{fp},t-k-2} y_{t-k-1}]^2,$$

performance of extrapolative rule:

$$U_{\text{e},t} = -\sum_{k=0}^{\infty} \omega_k [y_{t-k-1} - \tilde{E}_{\text{e},t-k-2} y_{t-k-1}]^2.$$

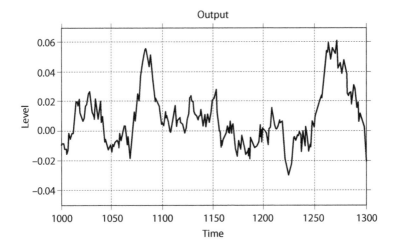

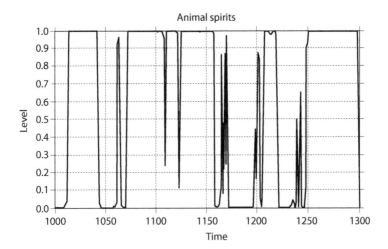

Figure 7.1. Output gap and animal spirits in three-agent model.

The corresponding probabilities of using the three rules now are:

$$\alpha_{\text{fo},t} = \frac{\exp(\gamma U_{\text{fo},t})}{\exp(\gamma U_{\text{fo},t}) + \exp(\gamma U_{\text{fp},t}) + \exp(\gamma U_{\text{e},t})}, \qquad (7.4)$$

$$\alpha_{\text{fp},t} = \frac{\exp(\gamma U_{\text{fp},t})}{\exp(\gamma U_{\text{fo},t}) + \exp(\gamma U_{\text{fp},t}) + \exp(\gamma U_{\text{e},t})}, \qquad (7.5)$$

$$\alpha_{\text{e},t} = \frac{\exp(\gamma U_{\text{e},t})}{\exp(\gamma U_{\text{fo},t}) + \exp(\gamma U_{\text{fp},t}) + \exp(\gamma U_{\text{e},t})}. \qquad (7.6)$$

Thus instead of having only two forecasting rules, we now have three rules from which agents will select the one that has the best performance.

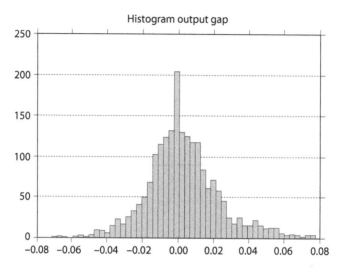

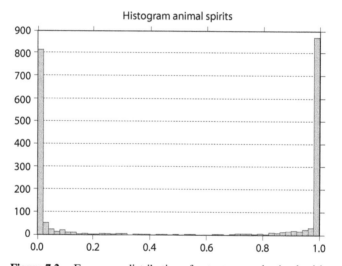

Figure 7.2. Frequency distribution of output gap and animal spirits.

The extended model was simulated in the time domain using the same calibration as in chapter 1. The results of a typical simulation in the time domain are shown in figure 7.1. The first panel shows the fluctuations in the output gap. We now obtain fluctuations that are more pronounced and protracted than in the two-agent model of chapter 1. This has to do with the fact that the animal spirits (the waves of optimism and pessimism) are more pronounced. We now redefine animal spirits to consist of the sum of the fractions of optimistic fundamentalists and positive extrapolators. These now reinforce each other producing stronger waves of optimism an pessimism. This is shown in the second panel of figure 7.1.

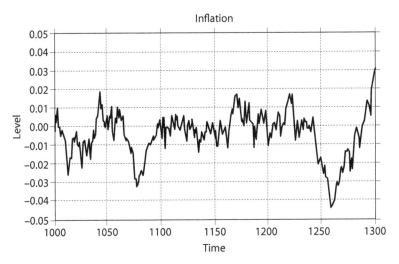

Figure 7.3. Inflation in the three-agent model.

In order to show the nature of the fluctuations in the output gap we also present the frequency distributions of the output gap and animal spirits. These are shown in figure 7.2. The results contrast with those obtained in the basic model in that the fat tails in the output gap movements are now more pronounced. The origin of these stronger fat tails is to be found in the much higher concentration of observations of animal spirits around 0 (extreme pessimism) and 1 (extreme optimism). Thus the biases (optimistic or pessimistic) in the fundamentalists' estimations of the equilibrium output gap together with the existence of extrapolators have the effect of reinforcing waves of optimism and pessimism, producing movements in the output gap that deviate even further from the normal distribution than in the simple two-agent model of chapter 1.

The results obtained for inflation are similar to those of chapter 1. We observe periods of tranquility (great moderation) in the movements of inflation (see figure 7.3). During these periods inflation remains very close to the inflation target set by the central bank (±1%). But suddenly inflation can tend to deviate substantially from the target. This happens when the inflation extrapolators tend to dominate the market. In this model these deviations are always temporary because the central bank uses the Taylor rule and thus increases the interest rate when inflation increases and vice versa.

7.2 Shocks and Trade-offs

How does the three-agent model perform when it is subjected to exogenous disturbances? We analyze this question now, and compare our results with those obtained in the basic model. We subjected the model to a positive productivity shock and

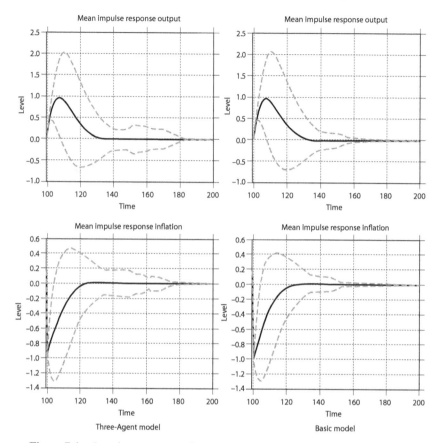

Figure 7.4. Impulse responses of output gap and inflation to productivity shock.

computed the impulse response of the output gap and inflation. In figure 7.4 we present the results and we also compare these with the impulse responses obtained (under the same conditions) in the basic model.

On the whole we obtain very similar impulse responses in the three-agent model as compared with the basic model. In both models the productivity shock leads to an increase in the output gap and a decline in inflation. In both cases there is considerable uncertainty about how the productivity shock is transmitted into the economy. We discussed this feature in chapter 2. It has to do with the fact that the model is sensitive to initial conditions. Different initial conditions (market sentiments) affect how the same shock is transmitted to the economy. From a comparison of the left- and right-hand panels in figure 7.4 we find that the uncertainty is even more pronounced in the three-agent model than in the basic model. This has to do with the fact that the three-agent model produces stronger waves of optimism and pessimism (animal spirits) than the basic model and stronger deviations from normality.

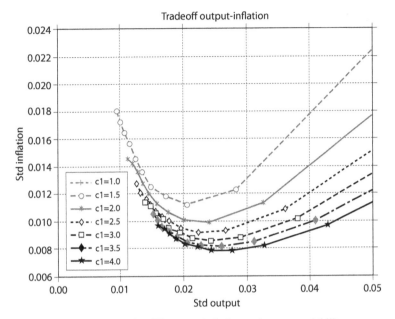

Figure 7.5. Trade-off between inflation and output variability.

Finally, we also calculate the trade-offs in our three-agent model in the same way as was done in chapter 3. We find the same nonlinearity in the trade-offs as in the basic model. We interpreted this nonlinearity to mean that there is scope for active stabilization of the output gap. This is the range in which the trade-off has a positive slope. In that range the central bank can by stabilizing output improve both inflation and output stability. This only works up to a point though. Too much output stabilization will bring us into the negatively sloped range in which any further attempt at stabilizing output leads to more inflation volatility. This point is reached when the Taylor output coefficient is increased above 0.5 (approximately). In general, when comparing the trade-off obtained in figure 7.5 with the trade-offs of chapter 3, we find that the nonlinearity is even more pronounced.

We also obtain the result of the basic model, which is that by reacting more strongly to inflation (an increasing Taylor inflation parameter, c_1) the trade-off improves (shifts downwards). This suggests that in this version of the behavioral model central banks can reduce both inflation and output volatility by keeping inflation close to its target.

Thus, overall the extension of the model to a richer menu of simple forecasting rules has kept the main results of the behavioral model pretty much unchanged. In fact, this extension has intensified the departure from the mainstream rational expectations models in different directions. It increases the departures from normality of the movements of the output gap. The main reason is that it intensifies the movements of animal spirits. This has the effect of creating more uncertainty about how exogenous shocks are transmitted into the economy, and creates more scope for output stabilization, without, however, reducing the need to maintain a credible inflation-targeting regime.

7.3   Further Extensions of the Basic Model

There are many more possible extensions of the model once we allow for different forecasting rules. In this section we present some results of an extension in another direction. In the previous models we assumed that agents use an extrapolative rule. We now drop this assumption and take the view that all agents use fundamentalist rules. We now consider three rules: an optimistic, a pessimistic rule, and a neutral one. Thus some agents use biased rules (either optimistic or pessimistic) and others use an unbiased estimate of the equilibrium output gap. The three rules become

$$\tilde{E}_t^{fo} y_{t+1} = a,$$

$$\tilde{E}_t^{fp} y_{t+1} = -a,$$

$$\tilde{E}_t^{n} y_{t+1} = 0.$$

The results of simulating this model are shown in figures 7.6 and 7.7.

This model produces similar results as the basic two-agent model, with animal spirits driving the cyclical movements in output. The latter, however, are less pronounced than in the previous three-agent model. This has much to do with the fact that in the present version of the three-agent model there are agents who have an unbiased view of the equilibrium output gap. These agents have a stabilizing influence on the fluctuations of output and inflation. Whether such agents exist in reality is another matter.

7.4   Conclusion

In this chapter we enriched the menu of rules that agents can use to make forecasts. We kept the same structure about how these rules are selected as in the previous chapters. We found that most of the results derived in the previous chapters are maintained.

Of course, one could go on extending the menu of possible heuristics that agents can use. Some extensions are surely necessary. For example, one would like to know how robust the model is when the number of rules becomes very large. Also, we have systematically presented the rules as a given menu from which agents can choose. But it is also possible for agents to create new rules and to experiment with these. This has not been done here. It is an area for further research. Such an extension would also reveal that the concept of equilibrium from classical models cannot easily be maintained.

It should also be mentioned that there is now a burgeoning literature on agent-based models that use a large number of agents with a large menu of heuristics.

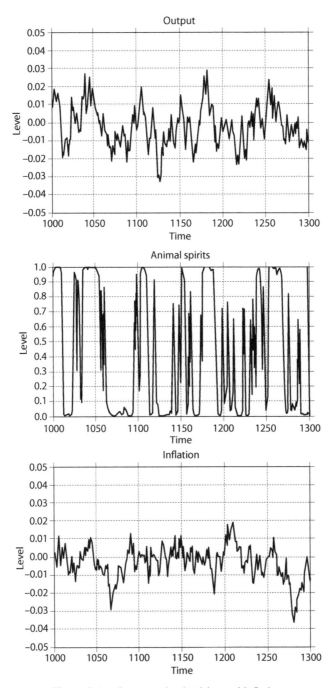

Figure 7.6. Output, animal spirits, and inflation.

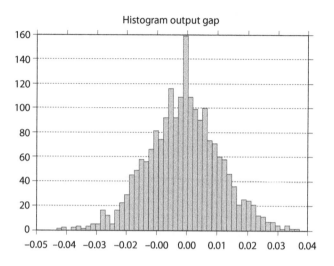

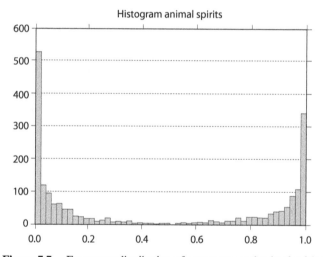

Figure 7.7.   Frequency distribution of output gap and animal spirits.

This literature was very much influenced by the early work of Schelling (1969) and Axelrod (1997). It has found increasing applications in economics (see Marimon et al. 1990; Delli Gatti et al. 2005; Colander et al. 2008; Farmer 2008; LeBaron and Tesfatsion 2008; Howitt 2008; Tesfatsion 2006). The common characteristic of these models is that they consist of autonomous agents following simple rules of behavior and interacting with many other agents producing complex outcomes. This is also the setup we used here. It is to be expected that new and exciting results will emerge from this literature.

8

Empirical Issues

8.1 Introduction

A theoretical model can only convince if it passes some form of empirical testing. This is also the case with the behavioral model discussed in this book. The problem in macroeconomics is how to devise a credible empirical test of the model. The history of macroeconomics is littered with examples of models which passed econometric testing procedures with flying colors, to be found wanting later.

The empirical testing tradition in macroeconomics has consisted in estimating an econometric model that embodies the equations of the theoretical model and then to perform dynamic simulations given the exogenous variables. Measures of goodness of fit then allowed the researcher to decide about the empirical validity of the theoretical model.

This approach is now severely criticized. First, it does not pass the Lucas critique as the estimated parameters of the structural model are not invariant with respect to the policy regime (Lucas 1976). Second, an attempt to estimate a small-scale model, like the one presented in this book, is likely to encounter problems of missing variables and incomplete dynamics. This is likely to lead to a misspecified model. Some researchers have reacted to this by adding autoregressive processes in the error terms as a cheap way to deal with these specification errors. We have argued that some of the existing DSGE models suffer from this problem. This approach is not attractive. The main reason is that it does not allow us to find out whether the model is rejected by the data or not (see Juselius and Franchi 2007). We will therefore not try to do this.

We will follow the approach of indirect inference, i.e., we ask what the predictions of the theoretical model are and confront these predictions with the data. Of course, it should be stressed from the start that a lot of uncertainty will continue to prevail about the empirical validity of the behavioral model.

Let us list the main predictions of the behavioral model.

1. Output movements are correlated with measures of optimism and pessimism, i.e., when market sentiments are optimistic (pessimistic) output increases (decreases).

2. Output movements are not normally distributed and show fat tails.

3. An interest rate increase leads to a temporary decline in output and inflation (as in other models). These effects, however, are time dependent (depend on market sentiments). This leads to different impulse responses depending on the timing of the shock.

We now check whether these three predictions are corroborated by empirical evidence.

8.2   The Correlation of Output Movements and Animal Spirits

The concept of animal spirits, i.e., waves of optimism and pessimism, has played a central role in the behavioral macroeconomic model presented in the previous chapters. The first question that arises here is whether there is an empirical counterpart for this concept. The answer is that there is, and it is widely used in day-to-day macroeconomic analysis. Many countries use survey-based consumer and/or business sentiment indicators as a tool with which to analyze the business cycle and as a predictive instrument.

The best-known sentiment indicator in the United States is the Michigan Consumer Confidence indicator, which has been in use since the 1950s. The first measures of consumer confidence were developed by George Katona in the late 1940s (see Katona 1951). Since then similar indicators have been implemented in a large number of countries (see Ludvigson (2004) and Curtin (2007) for an evaluation). Typically, sentiment indicators are constructed on the basis of a number of questions of how the individual perceives the present and the future economic conditions. Thus, these surveys produce two indices, one concerning present conditions, and one about future economic conditions. I will concentrate on the latter here, because this comes closest to the concept of optimism and pessimism used in this book, which is forward looking. The structure of these questions usually presents the individual with a discrete choice between good, bad, and neutral. An example from the Michigan indicator is the question: "Do you think that during the next twelve months, we'll have good times financially or bad times or are you uncertain? [good times/uncertain/bad times]." The answers are then transformed into an index by computing the divergence between "good times" and "bad times" answers.

The question that is addressed in this section is to what extent these sentiment indicators behave in a way that is consistent with our behavioral macroeconomic model. In figure 8.1 the Michigan Consumer Confidence indicator is shown, together with the U.S. output gap (quarterly data) during 1970–2009. The correlated movements of the sentiment index and the output gap are striking. The correlation coefficient was found to be 0.6. Note that in the simulations reported in chapter 1 the correlation coefficient between the output gap and the fraction of optimists was typically around 0.85. The lower correlation observed in reality is

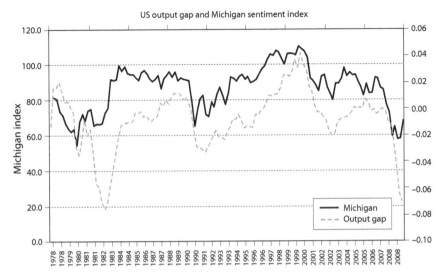

Figure 8.1. U.S. output gap and Michigan sentiment index (1970–2009).

Table 8.1. Pairwise Granger causality tests: behavioral model.

Null hypothesis	Obs	F-statistic	Probability
Output does not Granger cause optimism	1948	31.0990	5.1E-14
Optimism does not Granger cause output		32.8553	9.3E-15

Source: Calculated from the simulated output gap and animal spirits.

related to the fact that the survey-based sentiment indicators and the output gap have a lot of noise.

A typical feature of this correlation in the theoretical model is that the causality goes both ways, i.e., animal spirits affect output and output feeds back on animal spirits. We illustrate this by performing a Granger causality test on the simulated output gaps and the fractions of optimists obtained from the basic behavioral model of chapter 1 (see table 8.1). It shows that one cannot reject the hypotheses that animal spirits Granger cause the output gap and that the output gap Granger causes the animal spirits. Can one find the same structure in the relation between the observed GDP growth rates and the Michigan Consumer Confidence indicator? The answer is provided in table 8.2. It shows that one cannot reject the hypothesis that the Michigan Consumer Confidence indicator Granger causes the U.S. output gap and that the U.S. output gap Granger causes the Michigan Confidence indicator. Curtin (2007) has shown that in a majority of a sample of more than 50 countries one finds two-way causality between the confidence indicator and GDP growth (or another proxy for the business cycle).

Table 8.2. Pairwise Granger causality tests: U.S. data (1970–2009).

Null hypothesis	Obs	F-statistic	Probability
Michigan does not Granger cause GDP	123	15.83	0.00001
GDP does not Granger cause Michigan		4.83	0.0096

Source: Calculated from U.S. Department of Commerce, Bureau of Economic Analysis, and University of Michigan: Consumer Sentiment Index.

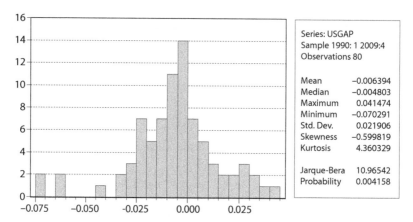

Figure 8.2. Frequency distribution of U.S. output gap.

8.3 Model Predictions: Higher Moments

In chapter 1 we showed that the behavioral model predicts that the output gap is not normally distributed and exhibits fat tails. This feature of the higher moments of the output gap is generated endogenously in the model. It is not the result of imposing such a feature on the stochastic shocks hitting the economy. We interpreted this result to mean that the model predicts that occasionally extreme movements in output can occur as a result of an endogenous dynamics. In chapter 1 we already confronted this prediction with data from the United States and concluded that indeed the distribution of the U.S. output gap during the postwar period was not normal. In this section we look at other countries, i.e., the United Kingdom and Germany. Unfortunately, the sample period is shorter and only starts in 1990. For the sake of comparability we also present the U.S. data for this shorter period. The results are shown in figures 8.2–8.4. They confirm what we found earlier, the output gap in these countries is not normally distributed (see the Jarque–Bera test, which rejects normality), and it exhibits fat tails. The latter means that the output gap is occasionally subjected to large changes that would not be observed if they were normally distributed.

One could object to this empirical analysis that the large shocks observed in the output gaps can also be the result of large exogenous shocks. In other words,

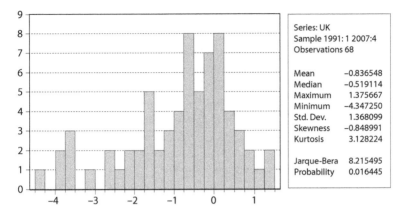

Figure 8.3. Frequency distribution of U.K. output gap.

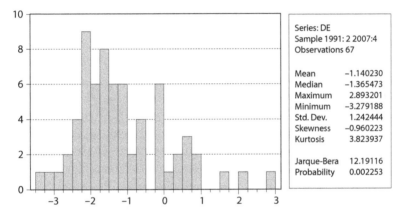

Figure 8.4. Frequency distribution of German output gap.

the evidence provided in figures 8.2–8.4 is also consistent with the view (implicit in DSGE models) that the macroeconomy does not produce large (nonnormally distributed) shocks, and thus that the observed large movements in output gaps must come from outside the model. Put differently, in the DSGE world large movements in output must be the result of large exogenous shocks.

The claim made here is not that the economy cannot sometimes be hit by large shocks, but that a theory that claims that large movements in output can *only* occur because of exogenous shocks is not a powerful theory. It necessitates finding a new exogenous explanation for every large boom and bust observed in output.[1] Put differently, for every boom or every bust a new story has to be told. Such a theory has very little predictive power. It amounts to a sophisticated story-telling

---

[1] For an illustration of this approach, see Favero (2001, pp. 73–75). Favero finds that there are many outliers in a VAR model of the U.S. economy, but interprets this to be the result of exogenous shocks (e.g., oil shocks). He then adds many dummies and, no surprise, the errors become normal.

exercise. Our theory allows for an explanation that is generated within the model. It is, therefore, more powerful.

We also observe from a comparison of figures 8.2–8.4 that not only are there fat tails, but also that the shape of the distribution is very different across countries. This implies that on the basis of the observations in these countries it is very unlikely that reliable statistical inferences can be drawn. This suggests that, as was noted in chapter 1, uncertainty in the sense of Knight is an important dynamic driving the macroeconomic movements.

8.4 Transmission of Monetary Policy Shocks

Empirical testing in macroeconomics has been very much influenced by Sims's (1980) seminal contribution (see Favero 2001). The basic idea is that theoretical models make predictions about the effects of policy shocks and that these predictions can be confronted with the data. This can be done by estimating a VAR of the macroeconomic variables and the policy variable. In the context of our model this consists in estimating a VAR of inflation, output gap, and the interest rate. This VAR then allows us to estimate an impulse response of inflation and output gap on interest rate shocks. This impulse response obtained from the data is then compared with the impulse response predicted by the theoretical model. It is important that, in doing so, the empirical impulse response is theory-free, i.e., does not use theory to impose identifying restrictions. After all, this approach is based on the idea of confronting theoretical predictions of the effect of a policy shock on inflation and output with the impulse response of inflation and output following a policy shock as detected from the data. In practice, this is not always easy to do, because restrictions on the parameters of the VAR must be imposed to be able to identify the impulse responses. The condition therefore has been to impose restrictions that use the least possible theory, or, put differently, that are used in the largest possible class of theoretical models. The Choleski decomposition (see, for example, Favero (2001) for explanation) is generally considered as the most theory-free set of restrictions.

Another popular set of identifying restrictions was proposed by Blanchard and Quah (1990). This consists in imposing restrictions on the long-term effects of demand and supply shocks based on theoretical insights. The latter are that demand shocks (e.g., a monetary shock) have only temporary effects. The problem with the Blanchard–Quah restrictions is that they exclude a priori a class of models that allow for multiple equilibria. In these models demand shocks can have permanent effects.

We now confront the theoretical impulses obtained from our behavioral model with the empirical ones. As a first step, we estimated a VAR model with three variables (output, inflation, and short-term interest rate) for the United States, using a Choleski decomposition (with ordering of inflation, output, interest rate). We then computed the impulse responses of output to an increase in the short-term interest

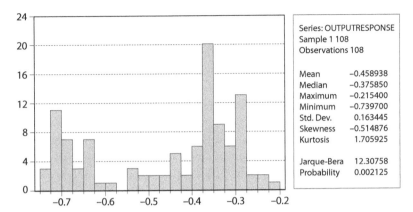

Figure 8.5. Distribution of short-term output response to shock Federal Funds rate.

rate (the Federal Funds rate). One of the main predictions of the behavioral model is that the impulse responses are very much influenced by the timing of the shock. We tested the empirical validity of this prediction by computing different impulse responses over different sample periods. We allowed for rolling sample periods of 30 years starting in 1972, and moving up each month. For each of these sample periods we computed the short-term output effect of an increase in the Federal Funds rate, where short-term refers to the effect after one year. We show the distribution of these short-term effects in figure 8.5. We find a wide range of short-term effects to the same policy shock (between -0.2% and -0.7% for a 1 standard deviation shock in the interest rate). In addition, we find that the distribution of these output responses is not normal. The Jarque–Bera test overwhelmingly rejects normality. We stressed in chapters 1 and 2 that this feature makes it very difficult for individual agents to make statistical inferences about the likely effects of a policy shock. On the whole the empirical results confirm the theoretical prediction of the behavioral model, i.e., the timing of the shock matters a great deal and affects how the same policy shock is transmitted into the economy. In addition, the nonnormality in the distribution of these shocks transforms risk into uncertainty (see chapter 2).

As in the case of the nonnormal distribution of the output gap, it must be admitted that the evidence of a nonnormal distribution of the short-term output effects of monetary policy shocks is not necessarily in contradiction with the DSGE model. In the framework of that model, the evidence provided here can be interpreted as arising from changes in policy regime. Ever since the famous Lucas critique (Lucas 1976), it has been well-known that changes in policy regime change the structural parameters of the standard demand and supply equations, and thus also change the transmission of policy shocks (the impulse responses). In this interpretation, the evidence of nonnormal distribution of the short-term output effects of a monetary policy shock is consistent with the view that there have been different changes in the policy regime during the sample period. These changes then produce nonnormal distributions of these effects.

Again we have two radically different interpretations of the same empirical evidence (which is not unusual in economics). The claim made in this book is that the interpretation given in the behavioral model is simpler than the one provided in the DSGE model. In the latter, the theoretical model predicts that, provided the policy regime does not change, a policy shock will always have the same effect. With noise in the data, the estimated effects of these shocks should be normally distributed. If we observe nonnormality, this must be produced outside the model, in this case by exogenous changes in the policy environment. Thus for every deviation from normality, the DSGE modelers must invoke a special event that has occurred outside the model. Such a model has no predictive power, because deviations from the predicted normality is always due to special circumstances. In contrast, in our behavioral model, nonnormality of the effects of policy shocks are not deviations from the rule, they are the rule.

We conclude that our behavioral model makes predictions that stand the test of the confrontation with the data. This does not mean, of course, that the empirical tests discussed here are in any way definitive. They should be considered as preliminary tests. Much more empirical testing will be necessary to elevate the behavioral model to the status of a serious alternative to the mainstream macroeconomic models.

8.5 Conclusion

Since its inception, booms and busts have characterized capitalism. The central issue in macroeconomics, therefore, is why these booms and busts in economic activity and in prices occur. Every macroeconomic theory must be capable of explaining these facts.

The explanation given by mainstream macroeconomics, in particular by new Keynesian rational expectations macroeconomics, fails to impress. In essence, the story told by mainstream macroeconomics is that these fluctuations arise because of large exogenous shocks. The latter have the effect of forcing rational agents to change their optimal consumption and production plans, but since they cannot adjust their plans instantaneously, prices and output adjust with lags. It is the combination of external shocks and slow adjustment that produces cyclical movements.

Thus, why did the world get into a recession in 2008–9? The answer given by the builders of the new Keynesian rational expectations model is that in 2007 a large external shock arose in the form of a sudden and unexpected increase in risk aversion. This change in risk perception then, like a hurricane, worked its way through the economy and produced a deep recession. In this sense mainstream macroeconomics has produced a "hurricane theory" of the business cycle.

The failure of mainstream macroeconomics to provide an endogenous explanation of booms and busts, in which a bust is the result of a previous boom, and a boom the result of a previous bust, has everything to do with the underlying paradigm of mainstream macroeconomics. This is the paradigm of the fully informed utility-maximizing agent who does not make systematic mistakes. Large booms or large busts can only be created by large external shocks to which these rational agents will then react.

I have argued that we need another macroeconomics that has the ambition of developing an endogenous explanation of the business cycle. I have tried to do so in this book. The behavioral model developed in this book allows us to better understand the recent macroeconomic developments in the world. The "Great Recession" of 2008–9 was not the result of an exogenous shock but resulted from excessive optimism that built up before 2008 and led to unsustainable consumption and investment. When the turnaround occurred, pessimism set in and led to a deep recession.

The behavioral model developed in this book was based on an enlarged concept of rationality. In mainstream macroeconomics, rationality is narrowly defined as utility maximization of agents who do not exhibit cognitive limitations, and as a result can solve incredibly complex problems of optimization and information processing. The starting point of the behavioral model presented in this book is that agents have limited cognitive abilities. These limitations force them to use simple rules (heuristics). Rationality was then introduced as a willingness of agents to learn by switching to alternative rules in order to improve their performance. Thus, moving away from the narrow rationality concept of mainstream macroeconomics does not imply that one is condemned to model irrationality where everything becomes possible.

References

Adjemian, S., M. Darracq Pariès, and S. Moyen. 2007. Optimal monetary policy in an estimated DSGE-model for the euro area. Working Paper 803, European Central Bank.

Akerlof, G., and R. Shiller. 2009. *Animal Spirits. How Human Psychology Drives the Economy and Why It Matters for Global Capitalism.* Princeton University Press.

Anderson, S., A. de Palma, and J.-F. Thisse. 1992. *Discrete Choice Theory of Product Differentiation.* Cambridge, MA: MIT Press.

Anufriev, M., T. Assenza, C. Hommes, and D. Massaro. 2009. Interest rate rules and macroeconomic stability under heterogeneous expectations. CeNDEF, University of Amsterdam.

Axelrod, R. 1997. *The Complexity of Cooperation: Agent-Based Models of Competition and Collaboration.* Princeton University Press.

Azariadis, C. 1981. Self-fulfilling prophecies. *Journal of Economic Theory* 25:380–396.

Azariadis, C., and R. Guesnerie. 1986. Sunspots and cycles. *Review of Economic Studies* 53:725–738.

Ball, L., G. Mankiw, and R. Reis. 2005. Monetary policy for inattentive economies. *Journal of Monetary Economics* 52:703–725.

Bean, C. 2003. Asset prices, financial imbalances and monetary policy: are inflation targets enough? In *Asset Prices and Monetary Policy* (ed. S. Richards and A. Robinson). Proceedings of a Conference, Reserve Bank of Australia.

Benhabib, J., and R. E. A. Farmer. 1994. Indeterminacy and increasing returns. *Journal of Economic Theory* 63:19–46.

Bernanke, B. 2003. Monetary policy and the stock market. Public Lecture, London School of Economics, October 9.

Bernanke, B., and M. Gertler. 1995. Inside the black box: the credit channel of monetary transmission. *Journal of Economic Perspectives* 9(Fall):27–48.

Bernanke, B., and M. Gertler. 2001. Should central banks respond to movements in asset prices. *American Economic Review* May, pp. 253–257.

Binder, M., and M. H. Pesaran. 1996. Multivariate rational expectations models and macroeconomic modeling: a review and some results. In *Handbook of Applied Econometrics: Macroeconomics* (ed. M. H. Pesaran and M. Wickens). Amsterdam: North-Holland.

Blanchard, O., and S. Fischer. 1989. *Lectures on Macroeconomics.* Cambridge, MA: MIT Press.

Blanchard, O. J., and D. Quah. 1990. The dynamic effects of aggregate demand and supply disturbances. NBER Working Paper Series 2737.

Bordo, M., and O. Jeanne. 2002. Monetary policy and asset prices. *International Finance* 5:139–164.

Borio, C., and W. White. 2004. Whither monetary and financial stability? The implications of evolving policy regimes. BIS Working Paper 147.

Branch, W., and G. Evans. 2006. Intrinsic heterogeneity in expectation formation. *Journal of Economic Theory* 127:264–295.

———. 2007. Model uncertainty and endogenous volatility. *Review of Economic Dynamics* 10:207–237

Branch, W., and G. Evans. 2011. Monetary policy with heterogeneous expectations. *Economic Theory* 47:365–393.

Branch, W. A., and B. McGough. 2008. Replicator dynamics in a Cobweb model with rationally heterogeneous expectations. *Journal of Economic Behavior and Organization* 65(2):224–244.

Brazier, A., R. Harrison, M. King, and T. Yates. 2008. The danger of inflating expectations of macroeconomic stability: heuristic switching in an overlapping generations monetary model. *International Journal of Central Banking* 32:2428–2452.

Brealy, R., and S. Myers. 1984. *Principles of Corporate Finance*, 2nd edn. McGraw-Hill.

Brock, W., and C. Hommes. 1997. A rational route to randomness. *Econometrica* 65:1059–1095.

Bullard, J., and K. Mitra. 2002. Learning about monetary policy rules. *Journal of Monetary Economics* 49:1105–1129.

Burda, M., and C. Wyplosz. 2009. *Macroeconomics. A European Text*, 5th edn. Oxford University Press.

Calvo, G. 1983. Staggered prices in a utility maximizing framework. *Journal of Monetary Economics* 12(3):383–398.

Camerer, C., and D. Lovallo. 1999. Overconfidence and excess entry: an experimental approach. *American Economic Review* 89:306–318.

Camerer, C., G. Loewenstein, and D. Prelec. 2005. Neuroeconomics: how neuroscience can inform economics. *Journal of Economic Literature*, 63(1):9–64.

Cecchetti, S., H. Genberg, J. Lipsky, and S. Wadhwani. 2000. Asset prices and central bank policy. *Geneva Reports on the World Economy*, vol. 2. International Center for Monetary and Banking Studies, Geneva, and CEPR, London.

Chari, V., P. Kehoe, and E. McGrattan. 2009. New Keynesian models: not yet useful for policy analysis. *American Economic Journal: Macroeconomics* 1(1):242–266.

Christiano, L., M. Eichenbaum, and C. Evans. 2001. Nominal rigidities and the dynamic effects of a shock to monetary policy. NBER Working Paper 8403.

Christiano, L., R. Motto, and M. Rostagno. 2007. Shocks, structures or monetary policies. Working Paper 774, European Central Bank.

Clarida, R., J. Galí, and M. Gertler. 1999. The science of monetary policy, a new Keynesian perspective. *Journal of Economic Literature* 37:1661–1707.

Colander, D., P. Howitt, A. Kirman, A. Leijonhufvud, and P. Mehrling. 2008. Beyond DSGE-models: toward an empirically based macroeconomics. *American Economic Review, Papers and Proceedings* 98:236–240.

Curtin, R. 2007. Consumer sentiment surveys: worldwide review and assessment. *Journal of Business Cycle Measurement and Analysis*, pp. 1–37

Damasio, A. 2003. *Looking for Spinoza, Joy, Sorrow and the Feeling Brain*. Orlando, FL: Harcourt.

Dawkins, R. 2009. *The Greatest Show on Earth. The Evidence for Evolution*. Simon and Schuster.

De Grauwe, P., and M. Grimaldi. 2006. *The Exchange Rate in a Behavioral Finance Framework*. Princeton University Press.

De Grauwe, P., and D. Gros. 2009. A new two-pillar strategy for the ECB. CEPS Policy Briefs, Brussels.

Della Vigna, S. 2007. Psychology and economics: evidence from the field. NBER Working Paper 13420.

Delli Gatti, D., C. Di Guilmi, E. Gaffeo, G. Giuloni, M. Gallegati, and A. Palestrini. 2005. A new approach to business fluctuations: heterogenous interacting agents, scaling laws and financial fragility. *Journal of Economic Behavior and Organization* 56:489–512.

De Long, J., B. Bradford, A. Shleifer, and L. Summers. 1990. Noise trader risk in financial markets. *Journal of Political Economy* 98:703–738.

Duffy, J. 2007. Agent-based models and human subject experiments. In *Handbook of Computational Economics*, vol. 2, ed. L. Tesfatsion and K. L. Judd. Amsterdam: North-Holland.

Evans, G., and S. Honkapohja. 2001. *Learning and Expectations in Macroeconomics*. Princeton University Press.

Evans, G., S. Honkapohja, and P. Romer. 1998. Growth cycles. *American Economic Review* 88:495–515.

Farmer, R. E. A. 2006. Animal spirits. In *Palgrave Dictionary of Economics*. London: Macmillan.

Fagiolo, G., M. Napoletano, and A. Roventini. 2008. Are output growth rate distributions fat-tailed: evidence for OECD countries. *Journal of Applied Econometrics* 23:639–669.

Fagiolo, G., M. Napoletano, M. Piazza, and A. Roventini. 2009. Detrending and the distributional properties of U.S. output time series. *Economics Bulletin* 29:4.

Farmer, R. E. A. (ed.) 2008. *Macroeconomics in the Small and in the Large*. Edward Elgar.

Favero, C. 2001. *Applied Macroeconomics*. New York: Wiley.

Farmer, R. E. A., and J.-T. Guo. 1994. Real business cycles and the animal spirits hypothesis. *Journal of Economic Theory* 63:42–73.

Gabaix, X., D. Laibson, G. Moloche, and S. Weinberg. 2006. Costly information acquisition: experimental analysis of a boundedly rational model. *American Economic Review* 96:1043–1068.

Galí, J. 2008. *Monetary Policy, Inflation and the Business Cycle*. Princeton University Press.

Gaspar, V., F. Smets, and D. Vestin. 2006. Adaptive learning, persistence and optimal monetary policy. Working Paper Series 644, European Central Bank.

Gigerenzer, G., and P. M. Todd. 1999. *Simple Heuristics That Make Us Smart*. New York: Oxford University Press.

Goodhart, C., and B. Hoffmann. 2004. Deflation, credit and asset prices. Working Paper, Financial Market Group, London School of Economics.

Goodwin, R. 1951. The nonlinear accelerator and the persistence of business cycles. *Econometrica* 19:1–17.

Greenspan, A. 2007. *The Age of Turbulence: Adventures in a New World*. London: Penguin.

Hayek, F. 1945. The use of knowledge in society. *American Economic Review* 35:519–530.

Hicks, J. R. 1950. *A Contribution to the Theory of the Trade Cycle*. Oxford University Press.

Holland, J. H., and J. H. Miller. 1991. Artificial adaptive agents in economic theory. *American Economic Review* 81:365–371.

Howitt, P. 2008. Macroeconomics with intelligent autonomous agents. In *Macroeconomics in the Small and the Large: Essays on Microfoundations, Macroeconomic Applications and Economic History in Honor of Axel Leijonhufvud*, ed. R. Farmer. Cheltenham: Edward Elgar.

Howitt, P., and R. P. McAfee. 1992. Animal spirits. *American Economic Review* 82:493–507.

Juselius, K., and M. Franchi. 2007. Taking a DSGE-model to the data meaningfully, the open access, open-assessment e-journal, Kiel Institute.

Kahneman, D. 2002 Maps of bounded rationality: a perspective on intuitive judgment and choice. Nobel Prize Lecture, December 8, Stockholm.

———. 2011. *Thinking, Fast and Slow*. London: Allen Lane.

Kahneman, D., and R. Thaler. 2006. Utility maximization and experienced utility. *Journal of Economic Perspectives* 20:221–234.

Kahneman, D., and A. Tversky. 1973. Prospect theory: an analysis of decisions under risk. *Econometrica* 47:313–327.

Katona, G. 1951. *Psychological Analysis of Economic Behavior*. New York: McGraw-Hill.

Keynes, J. M. 1936. *The General Theory of Employment, Interest and Money*. London: Macmillan.

Kindleberger, C. 2000. *Manias, Panics and Crashes. A History of Financial Crises*, 5th edn. Wiley

Kirchgässner, G. 2008. *Homo Oeconomicus: The Economic Model of Behaviour and Its Applications to Economics and Other Social Sciences*. New York: Springer.

Kirman, A. 1992. Ants, rationality and recruitment. *Quarterly Journal of Economics* 108:137–156.

Knight, F. 1921. *Risk, Uncertainty and Profits*. Boston, MA: Houghton Mifflin.

Kurz, M. 1994. On rational belief equilibria. *Economic Theory* 4:859–876.

Kurz, M., and M. Motolese. 2011. Diverse beliefs and time variability of risk premia. *Economic Theory* 4:877–900.

Kydland, F., and E. C. Prescott. 1982. Time to build and aggregate fluctuations. *Econometrica* 50:1345–1370.

LeBaron, B., and L. Tesfatsion. 2008. Modeling macroeconomies as open-ended dynamic systems of interacting agents. *American Economic Review* 98:246–250.

Leijonhufvud, A. 1993. Towards a not-too-rational macroeconomics. *Southern Economic Journal* 60(1):1–13.

Lucas, R. 1976. Econometric policy evaluation: a critique. *Carnegie-Rochester Conference Series on Public Policy* 1:19–46.

Ludvigson, S. 2004. Consumer confidence and consumer spending. *Journal of Economic Perspectives* 18(2):29–50.

Mankiw, N. G., and R. Reis. 2002. Sticky information versus sticky prices: a proposal to replace the new Keynesian Phillips curve. *Quarterly Journal of Economics* 117:1295–1328.

Marimon, R., E. McGratten, and T. Sargent. 1990. Money as a medium of exchange in an economy with artificially intelligent agents. *Journal of Economic Dynamics and Control* 14:329–373.

McCallum, B. 2005. Michael Woodford's *Interest and Prices*: a review article. Carnegie Mellon, Unpublished.

Milani, F. 2007a. Learning and time-varying macroeconomic volatility. Mimeo, University of California, Irvine.

———. 2007b. Expectations, learning and macroeconomic persistence. *Journal of Monetary Economics* 54:2065–2082.

Minford, P., and D. Peel. 1983. *Rational Expectations and the New Macroeconomics*. Oxford University Press.

Minsky, H. 1986. *Stabilizing an Unstable Economy*. New York: McGraw-Hill.

Orphanides, A., and J. Williams. 2004. Robust monetary policy with imperfect information. Board of Governors of the Federal Reserve System.

Pfajfar, D., and B. Zakelj. 2009. Experimental evidence on inflation expectation formation. Working Paper, Tilburg University.

Romer, D. 2005. *Advanced Macroeconomics*, 3rd edn. McGraw-Hill-Irwin.

Roubini, N. 2006. Why central banks should burst bubbles. Mimeo, Stern School of Business, NYU.

Sargent, T. 1993. *Bounded Rationality in Macroeconomics*. Oxford University Press.

Schelling, T. 1969. Models of segregation. *The American Economic Review* 59:488–493.

Schwartz, A. 2002. Asset price inflation and monetary policy. NBER Working Paper 9321.

Shell, K. 1977. Monnaie et allocation intertemporelle. CNRS Séminaire Roy-Malinvaud, Paris. (Title and abstract in French, text in English.)

Sims, C. 1980. Macroeconomics and reality. *Econometrica*, pp. 1–48.

Smets, F. 1997. Financial asset prices and monetary policy: theory and evidence. BIS Working Paper 47.

Smets, F., and R. Wouters. 2003. An estimated dynamic stochastic general equilibrium model. *Journal of the European Economic Association* 1:1123–1175.

———. 2007. Shocks and frictions in US business cycles. Working Paper 722, European Central Bank.

Solow, R. 2005. How did economics get that way and what way did it get? *Daedalus* 134(4):87–101.

Sutton, R., and A. Barto. 1998. *Reinforcement Learning. An Introduction*. Cambridge, MA: MIT Press.

Svensson, L. 1997. Inflation forecast targeting: implementing and monitoring inflation targets. *European Economic Review* 41:111–46.

Taylor, J. 1993. Discretion versus policy rules in practice. *Carnegie-Rochester Conference Series on Public Policy* 39:195–214.

Tesfatsion, L. 2006. Agent-based computational economics: a constructive approach to economic theory. In *Handbook of Computational Economics*, vol. 2: *Agent-Based Computational Economics*, ed. L. Tesfatsion and K. L. Judd, pp. 831–880. Handbooks in Economics Series. Amsterdam: North-Holland/Elsevier.

Thaler, R. 1994. *Quasi Rational Economics*. New York: Russell Sage Foundation.

Tversky, A., and D. Kahneman. 1981. The framing of decisions and the psychology of choice. *Science* 211:453–458.

Walsh, C. 2003. *Monetary Theory and Policy*. Cambridge, MA: MIT Press.

Wieland, V., T. Cwik, G. J. Müller, S. Schmidt, and M. Wolters. 2009. A new comparative approach to macroeconomic modeling and policy analysis. House of Finance, Goethe University of Frankfurt.

Woodford, M. 2003. *Interest and Prices: Foundations of a Theory of Monetary Policy*. Princeton University Press.

———. 2009. Convergence in macroeconomics: elements of the new synthesis. *American Economic Journal: Macroeconomics* 1(1):267–297.

Index

www.ingramcontent.com/pod-product-compliance
Ingram Content Group UK Ltd.
Pitfield, Milton Keynes, MK11 3LW, UK
UKHW030913230225
455446UK00005B/52